# BLACKBIRD
# DUST

ESSAYS, POEMS, AND PHOTOGRAPHS BY

## JONATHAN WILLIAMS

TURTLE POINT PRESS

Design and composition by Jeff Clark
at Wilsted & Taylor Publishing Services

*Library of Congress Cataloging-in-Publication Data*
Williams, Jonathan, 1929–
Blackbird dust : essays by Jonathan Williams. — 1st ed.
p. cm.
LCCN 00-130187
ISBN 1-885983-49-2
1. Poetry, Modern—History and criticism.
2. Poets, American. I. Title.
PS3545.I52966B53 2000 814′.6

*Printed in Canada*

FRONTISPIECE:
Jonathan Williams, Black Mountain College,
Black Mountain, North Carolina, 1955
*Photograph by Robert Creeley*

then i turned

and flew
down the dale

in the late
sunset light

the air
was full

of blackbird dust


*from a dreampoem*

# A NOTE

*Back in 1982 North Point Press issued a handsome, serviceable edition of my first book of essays,* The Magpie's Bagpipe *(title devised by Tom Meyer, who edited and introduced the book). Despite a ringing one-page review by John Russell in the* New York Times Book Review *and some 20 other excellent notices in magazines and newspapers, North Point was able to sell slightly less than one thousand copies in our broad land. They were forced to remainder the bulk of the 5000 copies printed. Good news, in its way, for the writer, because the cheap copies fell into the hands of students and beginning readers. Bad news for the publisher. In 1991 North Point "died of excellence," to use Guy Davenport's words.*

Blackbird Dust *is another celebration of Outsiderdom. Guy Davenport finds my writing "paratactic, peripatetic, and cathectic," and it would be rude to argue with such a seasoned assessment. The mix, as ever, involves food, drink, sex, sport, walking, manners, music, writers, artists, photographers—much that has been sternly isolated and sedulously ignored. I have tried to be as companionable, jocular, and curmudgeonly as possible in our poor literary times. Southern-fried bourgeoisophobes don't come along every day, so I must beg charity and forbearance.*

*Every piece in this knot-garden has been weeded and revised. I mention knot-gardens because I have a very here/there, in/out Celtic mind. Imagine a Tudor garden at a great English manor house. It will have little square, knotted, geometrical areas—flowers compartmentalized within low hedges of box. Like that, I tend to dart and swoop, and interlace one rinceau after another. I hope that the range of enthusiasms will atone, in part, for my tendency to pull out the banjo and play endless choruses of "Poor Jonathan Five Note." Meaning, I am a person with certain fierce adages always at the ready, and you will get Olson on form and Zukofsky on function jammed down your throat, world without end.*

*My old buddy Sandy McClatchy, who is as urbane, charming, and insulting as anyone I know, says, I remind him of the schoolyard bully, al-*

*ways kicking sand in the eyes of Robert Lowell, Helen Vendler, and The Old Eastern-Corridor Gang. But, I don't think I protest too much about the snarls and snares of our entertainment-clogged cloaca . . . I feel that I have to protect the Margins, because that's where I live. I really don't want $5000 from the Academy of American Poets ("prizes are for boys," said Charles Edward Ives). I don't want to be invited to Yaddo. I no longer want to be invited to join the Century Club, particularly since, with any luck, I may never have to go even one more time to New York City. I hope I would have the fortitude to say NO THANKS, if the phone from the MacArthur Foundation finally rang. "Sorry, guys, you waited just too long."*

*Alors, this epicurean knot-garden is now open for inspection. We hope Epicurus and other friends will come to call. ("A friend is a new self," avers G. Davenport.) Yet, as much as one longs for good, new readers, one cannot go nuts trying to figure out how few or many they might be. Basil Bunting makes the point very clear: "Readers are not what one writes for after one's got rid of the cruder ambitions." (What a terrible thing to tell a genial publisher.)*

**JONATHAN WILLIAMS**

Skywinding Farm
Scaly Mountain, North Carolina

# FOR TOM;

*and for new, young readers,*
*among whom are:*

**MICHAEL HENY**

**MICHAEL WATT**

**MICHAEL VON UCHTRUP**

**GREGORY HAYS**

**ANNE MIDGETTE**

**HARRY GILONIS**

**GREGORY O'BRIEN**

**WENDY KRAMER**

**JONT WHITTINGTON**

**GREVILLE WORTHINGTON**

**REUBEN COX**

**TIM DAVIS**

**THOMAS EVANS**

**JEFF CLARK**

**BRIAN BERGER**

**WARREN LIU**

**JONATHAN BOYD—**

*they read so well*
*they make me work much harder;*

*and not to forget*

**JAMES JAFFE,**

*the only bibliographer I know*
*who goes to the hoop!*

# CONTENTS

The Editor, *The New York Times Book Review*   1

Ernest Matthew Mickler (1940–1988)   3

Alfred Starr Hamilton, Poet   6

Paying Respects   10

"Coming Through Unfettered" as Ray Says   15

Feral & Sidereal   23

Meta-Fours   27

Amuse-Gueules for Bemused Ghouls   29

An Interview with Basil Bunting   37

The Hardy Boys Go to Work at Carmen Sutra's Bookstore   50

"I Don't Care If I Never Get Back"   53

Robert Duncan (1919–1988)   59

The Adventures of James Richard Broughton   62

A Garland for Ian Gardner   71

A Particularly Non-Arty Response to the Coracle Man   77

"We All Live in a Yellow Submaroon"   80

Bill Anthony's Greatest Hits, by William Anthony   85

Clerihews   87

The Clerihews of Clara Hughes   89

Clarence John Laughlin   95

Wild Gould Chase   100

Letter to the Editor of *The Spectator*   112

The Jargon Society  **114**

Paul Potts (1911–1990)  **123**

Henri Cartier-Bresson Says That "Photography Is
Pressing a Trigger, Bringing Your Finger Down
at the Right Moment"  **125**

And the Running Blueberry Would Adorn
the Parlours of Heaven  **143**

Joel Oppenheimer (1930–1988)  **154**

The Moon Pool and Others  **156**

Cocktales to Please Priapus  **167**

Making the Unsaid Say It All  **171**

"They Called for Madder Music and for Stronger Wine"  **174**

April Fool's Imitation-Type Test to While Away a Little Time  **177**

The Poetry of Work  **180**

"Who Knows the Fate of His Bones?"  **187**

"Back in Black Mountain, a Chile Will Slap Your Face . . ."  **193**

*The Talisman*, by Stephen King & Peter Straub  **196**

Homage to Art Sinsabaugh (1924–1983)  **199**

JCD  **208**

Virginia Randall Wilcox (1909–1991)  **210**

"Hiya, Ken Babe, What's the Bad Word for Today?"  **213**

James Laughlin (1914–1997)  **221**

Ronald Johnson (November 25, 1935–March 4, 1998)  **227**

James Harold Jennings (April 20, 1931–April 20, 1999)  **235**

Harry Callahan on Haguro-San  **240**

# THE EDITOR, THE NEW YORK
# TIMES BOOK REVIEW

Dear Sir,

I, too, am sobered by the revelation in Judy Karasik's article ("Take a Poet Home Today," May 11th) that the death of Mrs. Frederick Bowen in Bartholomew, Alabama, leaves only 83 poetry readers in the entire nation. I cannot find Bartholomew in my road atlas. I was hoping to locate it near the hamlet of Lower Peach Tree and then get in the VW and discover both the source of Helicon Creek and Alf the Sacred River.

I must tell you that 83 genuine poetry readers sounds much too high to me. I put their numbers at somewhere between the number of Ivory-Billed Woodpeckers (several sighted in Cuba recently) and the number of California Condors. Walter Lowenfels has made the clearest statement of the modern dilemma: "One reader is a *miracle*; two, a *mass movement.*" The only poetry readers I have unearthed lately lived near Pippa Passes, Dwarf, and Monkey's Eyebrow in Kentucky; at Odd, West Virginia; and at Loafers Glory and Erect, North Carolina.

Surely the collective efforts of 64,980 busy, untalented, published poets, plus the *National Entombment for the Arts,* plus the *Associated Arts-Demolition Councils of America* have convinced all sane people that modern-type poetry causes Herpes, AIDS, Leprosy, Lumbago, Terminal

1

Boredom, and/or Acne! I was, thus, horrified to find seven graduate students in Lexington, Kentucky, being taught the work of e. e. cummings and J. Williams by Professor Guy Davenport. They said they found me much more obscure than mr. cummings, because I persist in putting funny words like *Odilon* and *eidolon* in a poem. Happily, I had an hour to let them hear the noises the poems made. Now they say, it's all so easy a Yale Critic could understand (if not like) the results.

As the publisher of *White Trash Cooking,* may I offer one health tip to the clutch of recidivists who will persist in reading poetry no matter what. Always boil your poetry books in a pot likker made of alum, molasses, collards, and fat back. With any luck all the pages will say glued together, forever.

May Mnemosyne rub it on us!

Jonathan Williams

# ERNEST MATTHEW MICKLER

# (1940-1988)

This morning (November 16th) the news is that Ernie Mickler, genuine-book-author-feller of two of the most magnannygoshus works of the 1980s, *White Trash Cooking* and *Sinkin Spells, Hot Flashes, Fits and Cravins*, died yesterday of Kaposi's Sarcoma at his home in the Moccasin Branch section of Elkton, Florida. Ernie was 48. He leaves his collaborator and companion, Gary Jolley. A month ago it was the poet Joel Oppenheimer, who at least made it to 58, and died of a "nice" old-fashioned disease like lung cancer. Within months, two of the more arresting poets in California (Jack Sharpless) and London (David Robilliard) have been cut off in their thirties before more than a handful of other writers and friends knew what they were beginning to do.

We are back in the 19th century, where the folks who brought us the old élan vital, i.e., the friskier levels of Bohemia, were all dying of the pox (Baudelaire, Schubert, Wilde, Delius); or being wasted by consumption (Chopin, Keats, Firbank); or odd combinations of booze, boys, and lunacy (Rimbaud, Dowson, Poe). Think of things people lived with, feeling miserable most of their lives. Walt Whitman's obituary (1892) speaks of: "... pleurisy of the left side, consumption of the right lung, general miliary tuberculosis and parenchymatous nephritis ... a fatty liver, a huge stone filling the gall, a cyst in the adrenal, tubercular abesses involving

**3**

the bones, and pachymeningitis." The Anhedonists stayed at home, pretended to be straight-arrows, read the Gideon, and longed for the Dark Angel to get all those people who got more than they did.

*White Trash Cooking* came out of Nowhere-America like the wet, uninvited hound dog at the lawn party, sprinkling water and iconoclasm all over the culinary nobodies pretending to be somebodies. It soon had the likes of Alan Davidson (in *The Sunday Telegraph*), Neil Hanson (Editor of *The Good Beer Guide*), Harper Lee, *The New York Times*, *Vogue*, Helen Hayes, William Least Heat-Moon, Roy Blount, Jr., and Senator William J. Fulbright passing the collard greens and begging for more. A gentleman named Coleman Andrews, writing in the magazine *Metropolitan Home*, said *White Trash Cooking* was, *by far*, the best American cookbook of the century. The Jargon Society had to borrow from its board members to publish the first edition of 5000 copies. Over 600,000 have since been sold through the auspices of Ten Speed Press in Berkeley, California.

America turned out to have refined, finger-lickin, rustic peasants, just like France and Italy. We just call them folks. Some of their food was stunning. Some was killing. It went down a treat. Recently in Basel, Switzerland, a distinguished antiquarian bookseller told us of introducing "Tutti's Fruited Porkettes" and "Grand Canyon Cake" to his staid, suddenly enraptured guests. One imagines Erasmus washing down "Rack of Spam" with a good bottle of Alsatian Riesling. (Meister, may we suggest the 1983 Reserve from Colette Faller's *Domaine Weinbach* in Kaysersberg? Hit'll drink!)

Ernest Matthew Mickler was born in Palm Valley, Florida, a bastion of White Trash aristocracy. Said Ernie: "Where I come from in North Florida, you never failed to say "yes ma'm" and "no sir", never sat on a made-up bed (or put your hat on it), never opened somebody else's icebox, never left food on your plate, never left the table without permission, and never forgot to say "thank you" for the teeniest favor. That's the way the ones before us were raised and that's the way they raised us in the

4

South." After high school, he became a duo with Petie Pickette, writing and singing country music. They sang with top people like Mother Maybelle Carter, Roy Orbison, and Patsy Cline.

Later on, he talked his way into Jacksonville University and Mills College and obtained BFA and MFA degrees in their art departments. For years during his meanderings in the South, he filled paperbags with handed-down recipes from such mouth-watering towns as Flea Hop, Waterproof, Slap Up, Cut Off, Hot Coffee, and Burnt Corn. His correspondents included great unknown masters of the cookstove and iron skillet: Big Reba, Edna Rae, Sheba Spann, Mona Lisa Sapp ("You can turn this salad everyway but loose and it's gonna be good!"), Bonnie Jean Butt, and Retha Faye. Hillie Manes assured Ernie: "This Lemon Chess Pie is so good it'll make you drop yo drawers." I wonder if the *tarte au citron* I once experienced at Fernand Point's *Restaurant de la Pyramide* in Vienne was any better? It certainly cost more.

Well, a lot of fun and sass and gusto left us when Ernie went. He was a "natural man," as they say down South. He wrote like he talked, a kind of a-literate Eudora Welty. "The sun melted like butter over his sweetcorn thoughts," to use Irving Layton's wonderful words. His thousands of color snapshots are as plain, authentic, and tasty as his recipe for Cathead Biscuits. Ernest Matthew Mickler had a "gom" of friends—they spread from the old pals in Florida to the salivating outside world, which loved his two books. In three short years, he became an outlandish institution. There is a copy of *White Trash Cooking* on a library table in the Nymphenburg Palace in Bavaria. Bless his heart!

*(Unpublished, 1988)*

**5**

# ALFRED STARR HAMILTON, POET

Once upon a time, I used to know an honest, yet humble, advertising executive in Buckhead, Georgia, by the name of James Dickey. He was surely the only man in the Peach State who could talk about F. S. Flint, R. E. F. Larsson, Mina Loy—I mean *poets*, whether they were minor ones or major ones. He would get a wild good light in his eyes. Well, that was 17 years ago. Mr. Dickey, having run through the Poetry World like green corn through a cow, now masquerades as Sheriff Super-Jock, of Deliverance County, Jawja.

The Legend is depressing, and I wish he would stop it. But the ineffable public loves poets who are "all man" as much as it mindlessly devours the truth of headlines in the *National Enquirer*: **SPACE ALIENS TURNED OUR SON INTO AN OLIVE**. Despite testimonials to the contrary, Mr. Dickey doesn't think I can write a lick; and I don't trust a thing he says anymore (which is not a happy state to exist between two poets who once seemed to be friends). I bring him up, unkindly, because the uses of fame allow James Dickey to demand $3500 for a poetry reading. Even a remote institution of the higher learning like Catawba College, Salisbury, NC, thinks it's getting a bargain if they secure him from the agent for a grudging one grand.

I would like to suggest to Mr. Dickey (and all poets who swing and

6

sway before the public at the moment for appreciable amounts of cash —whether they be Holy Men or Migrained Academics) that they give a benefit reading for a poet they have never heard of, who never goes anywhere, who has never read any poetry since Edwin Markham. I'm talking about Alfred Starr Hamilton: 41 South Willow Street, Montclair, NJ 07042.

Mr. Hamilton is 61 years old. He pays $40 a month for a linoleumed cell in a rooming house. He goes to the A&P on Saturday night for the bargain chicken pieces, picks up cigarette butts, smokes a little Prince Albert, gets clothes from the Salvation Army, and asks for a pint of Four Roses when anyone comes to visit him (which is about twice a year). In 1964 his mother left him $7000. He has been surviving, somehow, ever since —in his oddly calm, disembodied, happy, desperate way. But, in the last letter of his I've had the heart to open, he was saying: "I have received a subpoena from a Newark court, for vagrancy. But I understand these subpoenas are not to be answered. I hope so."

The Jargon Society published *The Poems of Alfred Starr Hamilton* (with drawings by Philip Van Ever) in 1970, because he is an ignored caitiff; and an "original" poet, tuned in, like Blake or Dickinson, to a singular and moving world of words that he offers gladly to one and all. Nobody reviewed the book. Not one foundation or arts agency I have written to has made the slightest response to his plight. William Cole, the editor, is the only person in the United States who has bothered himself. He secured a small emergency grant of $250 from P.E.N., which is used up. One of these days we'll pay no attention to a snippet at the bottom of a column in the *Montclair Clarion*, to the effect that Mr. A. S. Hamilton, self-styled poet, has been declared redundant by the State of New Jersey and put away in some bin.

The older I get the less I am able to be charitable to charitable institutions like the Ford Foundation and the Guggenheim Foundation and the New Jersey Arts Council. Cyril Connolly had their mentality pegged long ago: "Everything for the milk bar, and nothing for the cow." You'll not find them hopping on the train and going to 41 South Willow Street to find out with their own eyes. They stick to the five poets a year that *Time* magazine knows the names of. Poetry in the agora is no different from any other hard-sell item. The ladies and gents of the coteries with fingers in all the pies are the ladies and gents who pull out what withered plums there are.

If I lose sleep over this, Alfred Starr Hamilton doesn't. His indifference to scorn and neglect make William Blake seem more worldly than he was. But, Mr. Blake had his engraver's job, his Kate, and his disciples. Mr. Hamilton has nothing, except the 10 poems a day that the Poem Fairy leaves under his pillow for typing out by lunchtime—if there's any lunch—, before he takes his walk to the Public Library to read the paper he cannot afford to buy. This could be the story of any of three million sad old men, but it isn't. It is the condition of one poet who deserves just a modicum of dignity from the Society of Deaf-Ears. Montclair! What a town for this to be happening in: Republican Montclair. He wrote: "Well, I lost a hand abroad, but that was a hand for punching a typewriter and they thought that would do. They didn't like me at all. They were full of swaggadocio. They wanted more swag instead of culture."

We have man looking out of a window, making poems up—thousands of them, year after year, putting them into shoe boxes. He simply needs about $2000 to scrape along on for this year, 1975. Assuming the worst (that poets, arts councils, critics, universities, foundations will not do the job they are there to do), is it asking too much for a few private persons reading this column to do the simple human thing? Viz., put a check or a money order in an envelope and send it to New Jersey.

Charles Olson, one of my masters, taught that "he who controls rhythm/controls!" Maybe that was way down in Russia, where eggs cost a dolla, according to the old Blues lyric. I doubt that even Orpheus, who could move those trees and melt those rocks in the days when poetry had alleged clout, could melt the ice-floes in the contemporary heart? Again,

8

Hamilton: "There are more than enough forest brambles and under-brush and real entanglements of all kinds. I guess they think I am im-mune? I'm not immune, I'm just out in the open. There aren't as many bees as there used to be."

(The New York Times Book Review, *April 13, 1975*)

# PAYING RESPECTS

The famous old places are grown quite obscure. For some time I have been trying to ferret them out." Kaemon, the painter, said that to Basho, the poet, in Oku-No-Hosomichi (*Back Roads to Far Towns*). If you are quite lucky, you can still find the way to Emily Dickinson's grave behind Burger King and the Gulf station in Amherst.

Poets are the sign-painters for Elysium. They are alive to add to beloved traditions and to celebrate the Great Dead. However, because it seems there are as few poets around worth killing as other people, it is sometimes Just Plain Folks who write the epitaphs. In fact, one of the great epitaphs of the Western world is a few yards off the Appalachian Trail as you hike along Iron Mountain in the country dividing North Carolina and Tennessee. A stone monument honors one Uncle Nick Grindstaff with these words:

LIVED ALONE
SUFFERED ALONE
DIED ALONE

Turns out Uncle Nick was a hermit ("they say he went to Harvard University, and then took to drink after his ladylove died out West") and lived on the mountain for over 40 years, with an old horse and a dog or

10

two. The citizen who kept the general store down in Shady Valley, Tennessee, where Uncle would buy his meal and bacon twice a year, wrote the words. Somebody had to. Nick Grindstaff was a special man, with a story no one ever quite knew. What gets me, of course, being the sanguine democrat I occasionally am, is that a shopkeeper, who probably never heard of the word *poet* or read a line of what they call "poetry" in his whole life, could get those words to work like that. Makes me think that Johnny Appleseed and Walt Whitman actually did plant friendship by the rivers of America when I see language that good. If anyone is thus emboldened to put on his L. L. Bean "Maine Guide Shoes" and traipse up to the Iron Mountain, please keep on along the Blue Ridge five or six days to the northeast. Climb to the cemetery above Marion, Virginia. You will feel you're in the God's Acre of *Our Town*, looking out over all the firmament. You'll stand before Sherwood Anderson's grave, carved by Wharton Esherick. The granite spiral bears the line:

### LIFE NOT DEATH IS THE GREAT ADVENTURE

During a quarter century of poetic folly, I have become more and more goliardic, peripatetic, and simply bizarre. Notice the increasing unworldliness in the answers to three famous American questions: (1) Where were you when Franklin Delano Roosevelt died? I was playing soccer at St. Albans School . . . (2) Where were you when Bobby Thomson hit the Shot Heard Round the World? I was helping Dan Rice build the science building at Black Mountain College . . . (3) Where were you the weekend of the Cuban Missile Crisis? I was walking in the English Lake District, looking for the graves of Beatrix Potter and Kurt Schwitters. . . . (I failed with both. Schwitters was reported to be in the churchyard at Ambleside. The stone is there, I failed to find it. He has since been exhumed and his body buried in Germany. Miss Beattie was definitely not at Troutbeck Church, as three ancient tweedy informants blithely assured me she was. Her ashes are scattered in a wood at the highest part of Hill Top Farm, her property at Sawrey near Hawkshead. Still, Troutbeck

Church is worth it for the lovely William Morris/Burne-Jones stained glass window in the chancel.)

Once I drove to a columbarium in Reno, Nevada, looking for a pigeonhole with Robinson Jeffers' name on it. I didn't find it. The ashes were later scattered on the Pacific—apparently, against California law at the time. The family had first shipped the body out of state, and then done what they wished to with the remains . . . Kenneth Patchen's ashes, too, are mixed with the ocean at Half Moon Bay . . . Marsden Hartley wished to be mingled with the confluence of the Kennebec and Androscoggin rivers in Maine. You can just about find the place in a seedy industrial quarter near Brunswick.

I must have by now 300 slides of the resting places of human beings I much revere and whose works and persons nourish me. I have Mr. Charles E. Ives in Danbury; Carl Ruggles in Arlington, Vermont; MacDowell at the Peterborough colony; Gottschalk in Greenwood Cemetery, Brooklyn; John Philip Sousa in the Old Congressional Cemetery in Washington, DC; Stefan Wolpe at the Springs near East Hampton, Long Island. But, not yet Stephen Foster, or Charles Tomlinson Griffes, or George Gershwin. Or, Scott Joplin, though I recently heard he is in St. Michael's Cemetery in Queens—not far from Whitman's birthplace at Huntington, not far from John Coltrane's grave.

Jazzmen's graves must be among the most elusive of all. Bunk Johnson's, in New Iberia, Louisiana, is unmarked. He is buried in a white Catholic cemetery through the collusion of Weeks Hall (the eccentric master of the great house called "The Shadows on the Teche") and the parish priest. Charlie Parker is buried in a black cemetery east of Kansas City. When I paid my respects, there were withered yellow chrysanthemums beside the grave, left, I found out, by Dizzy Gillespie and his quintet, who came out to the cemetery the week before and played dirges for Bird.

Is all this "morbid"? I hardly think so. It can only be moving and instructive to see H.D.'s stone in the Moravian acre at Bethlehem, Pennsylvania. Hilda Doolittle Aldington, it is. Or, Franz Josef Kline's in Wilkes-Barre. Or, Hart Crane's father's in Garrettsville, Ohio, with its mention of

### HAROLD HART CRANE, LOST AT SEA

on the west side of the monument . . . Sir Herbert Read's headstone, in the yew-filled yard of St. Gregory's Minster at Kirkdale on the North York Moors says

### KNIGHT POET ANARCHIST . . .

Charles Olson has a curious black slate, of the 17th century kind with *memento mori*, in the Catholic fishermen's cemetery in Gloucester, Massachusetts. The stone is crumbling already . . . Edith Sitwell's, William Morris's, Kenneth Grahame's, Walter Sickert's, and Stanley Spencer's stones are all wonderfully incised and lettered—and quite hard to find. (I have to go back to Grahame's in Oxford, because, stupidly, I didn't know that Walter Pater was within a hundred yards.)

Do not merely seek out "The Great." It meant something to me—and perhaps to them—to find Adelaide Crapsey in Rochester, and H. P. Lovecraft in eldritch and hyperborean Providence. Said Basho: ". . . hard to locate anything now, but that moment, seeing the thousand-year-old monument, brought back sense of time past. One blessing of such a pilgrimage, one joy of having come through, aches of the journey forgotten, shaken, into eyes." (That translation by Cid Corman, who has done so much to restore to us the live words of poets so monumental as Matsuo Basho.)

Who can tell me where Albert Pinkham Ryder lies? Or Ferdinand "Jelly Roll" Morton? Or Charles Demuth? Or Mary Cassatt? Or Grant Wood? Or Marin? Or Arthur Dove? Or Stieglitz? Or Henry Clews? Or Nathaniel West? Or James Thurber? Or George Ade? Or Arnold Schoenberg? Or Harry Partch? Or Raymond Chandler? Or Art Tatum? Or Charles Reznikoff? Or Lorine Niedecker? My address is simply P.O. Box

**13**

10, Highlands, North Carolina 28741. I'm likely to be at home, unless off on my next mission—an important one for latter-day scat-singers: the Rev. Charles Dodgson (Guilford, Surrey?); Edward Lear and his cat Old Foss (San Remo?); and Christian Morgenstern. (Someone suggests the grounds of Rudolf Steiner's Goetheanum, where he taught his anthroposophic doctrines, at Dornach in the hills outside Basel, Switzerland.) May some other pilgrim attend Eddie Guest and Poets Nice People Like. R.I.P.

( New York Times Book Review, *December 19, 1976)*

Addendum, 1999: Albert Pinkham Ryder, James Thurber, Jelly Roll Morton, Lewis Carroll, and Lorine Niedecker are in hand. I am still missing the others.

# "COMING THROUGH UNFETTERED"
## AS RAY SAYS

I t is an excellent thing to look at photographs in which, as Oscar Wilde must have observed, you get nothing but photography. That is, images in service to Seeing. Not in services to Sociology, The Class System, An Excess of Rationality, Cosmic Adumbrations, Self-Expression, Masculinity, Document, etc, etc. One constantly hears in England: "Art is not so important as People. Art is not so important as Life. Art is not so important as Nature. Art is Small Beer." Blimey. Is it as important as itself? By Bright Apollo and by Nicéphor Nièpce, let us declare that it is!

If a sign in a Ray Moore photograph says "Maxwell Road," you do not have to ask what it means. It means "Maxwell Road." If a graffito says "BILLY" either Billy wrote it, or Mary did, or Neddy did, or, maybe, his mate Mark did. (Already the romantical mind starts to complicate. Just leave it at "Billy" and look at it.) I have been reading a lot of Oscar Wilde lately and rediscover how bracing the great man can be on almost any subject: "Cows are very fond of being photographed, and, unlike architecture, don't move . . ."

There's an old dyslexic saying, "You can't turn a silk purse into a sow's ear." Sure you can. We do it all the time. Most of us view "the ordinary" with just about enough perception to keep from being run over by a milk lorry. I think I have seen that phenomenon referred to as "the economic determinism of vision," but you will pardon me if I eschew abstract nouns and the lingo of the academy. As the venerable Molly Kirkbride, knitter of Wensleydale, used to say: "Remember, we were nobbut browt up like bullocks." (How in the world could she have known about the photographs of Wynn Bullock?) I like prose to jump about, and dance and sing.

Ray Moore images demand that you pay them exactly the attention they are due. They are not "like a lot of stuff you see around these days." They aren't. He likes to shoot "what is there." The point is: what is there also includes what isn't there—except at this one, most luminous moment in the history of seeing. Look at the one called "BILLY." Ray doesn't climb up Great Gable to find a visionary image. It comes out of the play of light between a car's windscreen and a scruffy bit of building in northern Cumbria. Russell Edson, the fabulist, would take a long look at "BILLY" and muse: "The things we took for granted do not take us so."

Ray Moore is a man constantly informed by music. He was talking yesterday: "The idea of Schubert . . . this guy who seems to happen on collections of notes which equate with his sense of at-one-ness with the world. Very small and very big at the same time. He seems "to string it together", and make musical sense while drifting away from the formalities . . . Which is my problem in the books and the exhibitions. I can imagine using the same print in several places within the context of a show."

Ray Moore shares affinities with Harry Callahan, and that is very good company. In both you have quietude, acute sensitivity, the desire to photograph the commonplace common-ground of the world. Both are willing to follow the light without much apparent thinking about why they are doing so. The result, in each case, is a companionable democracy of content. I don't know what's there for Lord Longford, Mrs. Thatcher, or Joe Gormley? I don't see much moral uplift or blows struck in behalf of any damn class at all. We are back at the truth that art is use-

16

less indeed. Beauty of craft and feeling is useless, which is why there is so little provision for it in present-day societies. Your eyes could do worse than make a covenant with the likes of Ray Moore. Am I saying that art is one of the best ways to salvage one's days on this planet? Blame it on my Welsh ancestors and let's get back to images.

The North Carolinian/Cumbrian person writing these words sets up in life with the vocation of poet—the only thing more silly than being a photographer. I am neither authority nor critic. I am an "appreciator" of photographs, and that very much includes these by Ray Moore. What are poems for? Equally, what are photographs for? Louis Zukofsky, who knows better than most, says their purpose is *To Record & Elate*. I hope we agree, Ray Moore and I, that this insight strikes home with the most blinding clarity. Think about it.

The poet, being a man who stands by his words, offers a few in response to prints by RM:

> traces,
> often human,
> of something that happened,
>
> then things
> got very quiet . . .

■

> black rectangles at the base of the sky . . .
> three holes in the land, leading to what?

■

> one B&B sign
> in a million—
>
> who drew it?
> Auntie Agnes?
>
> the great unknown "naive" artist
> of Aspatria, Cumbria . . .

with her mind
full of kippered-Hittite calligraphy,
cabochons of amber from the sea,
and a secret sensuality . . .

■

dish towel,
loyal to Apollo,
hangs a load of
damp Cumbrians on
the washline
to atone for a toneless sky
and to dry
too.

■

it's
only a lens

passing on information
at an exact moment

coagulations of silver deposits
do not make "it" less a sheep,
or less "the truth"

■

the window frame
reads like
the back of
a Mackintosh
chair

■

a horse
has been strung
on a wire
attached to a telephone pole

and become
a piece of
finely cut, triangular,
pictorial pizza,
worth of Duccio di Buoninsegna
of Siena

(it was Duccio,
don't forget
who first said to
"Fats" Waller:
it don't mean
a thing
if it ain't got that
swing)

■

on the pony
is the map of
Fetlar in the
Shetlands,
seen from the skies
over Vord Hill
by the snowy owl

■

somebody,
probably Hermes,
god of waysides, crossroads, messages,
poetry & theft,

is always
adding and subtracting
rectangles
from Ray Moore landscapes:

road signs,
opening in fence walls,
flat paper bags,
the low kerb
around a grave,
bits that make oblique angles to the left
and flatten out on
the picture plane

■

one loves only form
and form only comes
into existence when
the thing is born

born of yourself, born
of hay and cotton struts,
of street-pickings, wharves, weeds
you carry in, my bird

of a bone of a fish
of a straw, or will
of a color, of a bell
of yourself, torn . . .

—which is
Charles Olson,
at the beginning of *The Maximus Poems*,
and it says a lot of
what is to be said
about Ray Moore's photographs,

before we put on our
wide-eyed wellington boots
and set forth for any damn place at all
with this black-and-white song in our hearts
and a lilt in both ears—

so you wanna lyric?
you gotta lyric!
whatsa matta you?

■

a little sky,
a telephone pole,
three wires,
55 felt-tip pretend-sheep,
a bush, some bits of grass,

snow, a hill,
and this large bloke
with the guise
of a not-so ancient mariner,
the eye of a gull,
and a camera,
which

"only connects"

■

Looking through this selection of prints by Raymond Moore should indi-
cate at least two things. Excuse me, let's make that three things: (1) En-
gland has a photographer of international stature on its hands, so it's
about time the locals paid more attention . . . (2) if you go to the English
Lakes to see "the sights," there are plenty more not recorded by Mr.
Wordsworth of Cockermouth—the fore-shore at Allonby and industrial

bits of Maryport for a start . . . (3) there are, finally, only eyes in all heads, to be looked out of . . .

Do we always take the same photograph, or write the same poem? The answer is yes or no, like most answers. "I am written" says Rimbaud. "Eeee, I'm tupped, buggered, shuttered, shattered, clicked, and snapped," a Cumbrian hill farmer with a warm Mamiyaflex might say.

*(Afterword to* Murmurs at Every Turn, the Photographs
of Raymond Moore, *Travelling Light, London, 1981)*

Coda: Ray Moore died on October 13, 1987. I wrote an obituary for *The Independent* in London and would like to quote the last paragraph: "I probably should have sat this sad evening and listened to his favorite, Franz Schubert, that late piano sonata, D. 960. Instead, I went for something even bigger, because Raymond Moore was a world-class figure—and it's the end of the day and the British (and the Americans) should realize this. The only place to go was to the Adagio of the Bruckner *Eighth Symphony,* where light of that sort fell on earth for the first time. To join Schubert and Bruckner in their luminous refrain: the Light in the Uplands of England has lost the man who saw it like no one else."

# FERAL & SIDEREAL

It is strange to be living here in Dentdale, the "terrestrial paradise," without the anticipation of visits from the Venerable Baz, fresh from Northumberland, chugging up the fell in his decrepit Daf motorcar, coming from under the big horse-chestnut tree, calling for a chair by the fire, an ashtray, WHISKY!, and maybe a little apple tart. For fifteen years he came regularly to Corn Close in the Cumbrian Pennines, three miles up the River Dee above Brigflatts Meeting House. (The locals spell it with one g; Basil with two.) Twice, he lived on his own at Corn Close, after being uprooted at Wylam and Greystead.

Interesting how his words resonate at odd, particular moments. Today, July 1, 1985, thirty-nine American hostages left Lebanon. And I happened across these words from Basil to Louis Zukofsky in 1953: "Reverting to the West has made me more convinced than before that we've got to learn almost everything from the East (which, to the measure of my limited experience, is the lands of Islam) before there's a chance of any peace of mind or dignity for most of us. And that's a way of saying to hell with material welfare, and, logically, of all the laws and reforms, and adages designed to procure it." Certainly, material things held little interest for Bunting. He lived almost poorly on bread and cheese, a bit of curry and rice, fruit pies, tea, bitter beer, and the odd bottle of single malt, when affordable. He had the simplest wardrobe and no possessions of interest or value except for his small, treasured library.

All the poems that Basil Bunting wanted collected for the pleasure of generations of "unabashed boys and girls" are in this volume. The one addition to the Oxford University Press edition of 1978 is *Perche no spero* (Second Book of Odes 12). Jennifer Moyer and Britt Bell, the publishers, spent an afternoon with BB at Whitley Chapel only ten days before his death, and they have heeded his wishes: just the *one* extra poem.

Once in a rare while you meet an unabashed boy or girl walking abroad on the British Isles, but they have seldom been taught enough reading or cultural skills to handle a poet as complex in his craft as Basil Bunting. Some of the patterning he loved in the Persian poets came to him out of his own Celtic/Anglic Northumbrian heritage: the sculpted crosses at Bewcastle and Ruthwell, the *Codex Lindisfarnensis.* He admired, as he said, their intricacy, and their "terseness and limpidity." Back in the 1930s he had almost no readers: "The intelligent reader in England is the frequenter of two small public-houses in Bloomsbury, plus a few idiosyncratic scholars in the provinces." In the 1980s the adjective he used to describe the British literary scene was *squalid.* And still: ridiculously few readers. Patience, little boke! They will come.

How to read Bunting? First of all, give it time; give yourself time. I still haven't read every line in the *Collected Poems* after 34 years of reading BB. I feel the need to hold something back for later years, as I do with the totality of the Brahms chamber music, or the Fauré chamber music, or with hundreds of harpsichord sonatas by Domenico Scarlatti. In the meantime, you might develop your reading in the poets that Bunting listed as Masters of the Art: Homer, Ferdosi, Manucheri, Dante, Hafez, Malherbe, Aneirin, Heledd, Wyatt, Spenser, Sidney, and Wordsworth. The last four, to make it easier, even wrote in English. (BB and I exchanged extensive words on all this in the 5th issue of the magazine *Conjunctions.*)

Bunting wrote in 1928: "No art depends principally or even very largely on its appeal to the intellect, and in the Age of Reason itself Pope was preferred to Young for melody, not for sense." However, for those who wish a near word-by-word analysis of *Briggflatts*, there are precise, diligent scholars about like Professor Eric Mottram to read in *Basil Bunting (Man & Poet)*.

Poets always argue about sound and sense, about "meaning." I like the lines by William Carlos Williams:

> I wanted to write a poem
> that you would understand.
> For what good is it to me
> if you can't understand it?
> But you got to try hard—

But, late in his life, confronted by the difficult sonic boom in Charles Olson's *Maximus*, Williams asked me in a letter: "How do you expect anyone to *understand* what he hasn't first *heard*?" Bunting would very much agree. Get the music in your head.

Another way to "read" Basil Bunting: walk the Pennine Way from Gargrave in the Aire Gap; over Stainmoor and its memories of Eric Bloodaxe; along the Roman Wall; over the Cheviots to Kirk Yetholm on the Scottish Borders. Nothing else compares to seeing, hearing, breathing the air of the landscape the man lived in. Sit in the silence of Brigflatts Meeting House some Sunday morning. Eat some Blue Wensleydale cheese and havercake. Have a few drams of Glenfiddich.

Peewit and curlew, clint and gryke, bear garlic and may, glishy slutch and Roman wall—these are certainties of the music. From these come variations and descant, one human being to another.

There was something sidereal about Basil Bunting; something feral as well. He could be remote as the stars he regarded over the Pennine Dales. He occasionally twinkled like them, but mostly kept silence . . . He loved the company of the red weasel by the beck . . . He composed his words as carefully as hill farmers build blue rag into dry stonewalls . . .

Men he endured, because now and then they also got their words right —when they were being unabashed ... Bunting's severity-cum-wit; no one else seems to have it, and that's what I shall miss most from this great man. *Great*, a somewhat too-human word, not often one that stars and weasels and stones bandy about.

*(Introduction to* The Collected Poems of Basil Bunting, *Moyer Bell Limited, Mt. Kisco, New York, 1985)*

# META-FOURS

The poet's fascination with his dotty invention, the *meta-four*, continues. It's only "rule" is that each line have four words. All punctuation and capitals are eliminated except for possessive apostrophes. The result (when it works) turns sense into nonsense and gets the mind so off-stride that you don't know whether you're coming or going. And you don't distinguish "prose" from "poetry." There is the ancient local limerick:

> There was a young bugger from Dent,
> whose cock was so long that it bent.
> To save himself trouble,
> he put it in double—
> and instead of coming, he went!!!

That's the idea.

Today's huckster now has about 15 seconds in which to sell soap—30 seconds strain the attention of the couch-potato. The wastrel poet (a no-goodnik with nothing to sell to any appalled American mall-rat) may not have but 5 seconds. He therefore alerts his words: you guys better creep in, crap, and creep out, like starting now: DO IT!

Judith Thurm gives good advice: "Start as near the end of a poem as you can."

The lines in a meta-four make sure that you do as much work as the writer did—maybe even more. Few will be willing, but the poet aspires to reach no one else. "Cromwell, I do charge thee, Flench from ambition. By that sin fell the angels," etc.

# AMUSE-GUEULES
# FOR BEMUSED GHOULS

good titles occur to
me all the time
like i have a
nephew who is a
proctologist from greer south
carolina and other poems

### HOMAGE TO LEE SMITH

one-eyed jesse waldron lives
all by hissef up
in the paw-paw gap

■

justine poole always says
fuckin' is fine as
far as it goes

two jewish ladies meet
in central park one

of them has a
new baby in a
carriage what's the baby's
name says one it's
shelley says the other
how nice that you
named her after a
famous poet shelley temple
was a famous poet

## CHARLIE RESNICK

bloke who played the
piano like a man
with no arms monk
that's him thelonious monk

and then sage heraclitus
said sagely oxen are
happy when there're lots
of peas to eat
he was perhaps the
first ever to notice
and hopefully the last

## PERSONS IN PARADISE GARDENS

what were they all
but skeletons given a
few years of life

### GARY GARDEN REPORTS FROM
### THE COFFEE SHOP IN SYLVA

whatzit you readin' carden
jonathan williams izat the
funny feller you must
be thinking of winters
hell yes down to
20 degrees this morning


### CORONATION STREET

and it's me that's
lost me job and
all you want to
think about is a
bit of the rumpy-pumpy


### RIBBLESDALE

ee you booger thou
doant know a lunkie
from a smoot hole
or a thirl go
play with yerself you
terrible little man you


mother said can't you
play something christmasy i
said well i just
played you the complete
nutcracker by michael tilson
thomas last year i
tried delius's walk to

**31**

the paradise garden and
she said can't you
play something pretty well
it is very hard
to please your mother

what if i tried
leroy anderson sleigh ride
might ring the gong
but then she'd say
don't you have any
strauss waltzes and i'd
say well maybe tomorrow
i need some sleep
we'll start with arnie
schoenberg's gurrelieder and get
that danube really blue

chasing some high cheese

## A MOCK-MORRIS
## FOR GAEL TURNBULL'S 70TH

arnold bax once said
famously that one should
do everything with the
obvious exceptions of incest
and morris dancing the
only one i know
who did otherwise was
the one-off percy grainger
let's offer our old

song & dance man
a toast more power
to your legs cheers

ask in secaucus is
a pork's ass pork

this is classic stuff
so these two yentas
are visiting in miami
beach for the first
time molly says ester
i want to ask
you something serious have
you been through the
menopause molly so slow
down already i haven't
even been through the
fountain blue and ester
the word is it's
tchotchkes to die for

### HYLOCICHLA MUSTELINA

thoreau says of the
wood thrush whenever a
man hears it he
is young and nature
is in her spring
whenever he hears it
it is a new
world and a free

country and the gates
of heaven are not
shut against him but
take it to a higher
plateau nearly six in
the morning the wood
thrush wakes you with
a boy's willing cock
in your hand higher
or lower mr thoreau

### JIMMY ROWLES (1918–1996)

a voice like a
canoe being dragged slowly
across an abandoned road

there's a great joke
in thomas adcock's new
detective novel devil's heaven
you know the definition
of an irish homosexual
it's a mick who
prefers women to whiskey

### LA GRANDE CUISINE CORNICHE

soggy ratty tatty oggy

### BIG ERMA

i might be too
old to cut the
mustard but i can
still lick the jar

jeffrey bernard put an
advert in the spectator
veteran alcoholic diabetic amputee
requires sympathy fuck aye
he'll be lucky chuck

a celadon-colored velvet armchair

dear elvis thank you
for carpeting all the
ceilings of our hearts

but this time you
hold the pigeon and
I'll shit on it

one of those florida
towns where homeless teenagers
with firehose dicks prowl
the streets at dusk
counting on the extreme
kindness of many strangers

smash hits features boyzone
every issue a recent
offer of the underpants
of take that heartthrob
mark owens worn and
unwashed received 300,000 applications

an extraordinary explication of
family values i mean

the ones that really
matter how can you
tell when your sister's
having her period well
says little brother it's
when your dad's dick
tastes different so where
is mom in all
this where she's out
with the local militia

**REAR-WINDOW STICKER
IN THE SEDBERGH CAR PARK**

overtake me and i'll
follow you home and
shit in your slippers

**B. B. KING**

nobody loves me but
my mama and she
may be jivin' too

so life goes on
very much like a
piece by morty feldman

*(Some of these meta-fours have appeared as Number 40 in the Backwoods
Broadsides Chaplet Series, edited & published by Sylvester Pollet in
Ellsworth, Maine. Many thanks to Mr. Pollet for permission to reprint.)*

# AN INTERVIEW
# WITH BASIL BUNTING

## PRE-AMBLE

If I were to give up (in disgust) the habit of writing poems and essays, because the literary world is simply too pig-ignorant, flash, and debased to think about, I could easily become a *cicerone* for foreign pilgrims wishing to explore the British Isles. Not so much the usual stuff but genuine *très soignée* oddities tucked back in the countryside: viz, Sarah Losh's remarkable church (1844) in the village of Wreay in Cumbria. ("Why go there?" asks Dan Archer. "Nobody in Ambridge, or Des Moines, Iowa, will have heard of it.") But, literature continues to grab me by the short 'aires. And there are still one or two poets as quizzical and interesting as Basil Bunting.

Pound wrote the *Guide to Kulchur* for him and Louis Zukofsky, "strugglers in the desert." At 83 he remains a nomad and a man of the desert in very damp Northumberland. He long ago gave up the idea of wealth and urbanity for his peculiar version of freedom in the depths of the countryside. There is something inhuman about this atheistic Quaker, this attender of Brigflatts Meeting House since 1912. He abominates the Middle-Class and claims he has never been able to afford its toys: the cameras, the stereos, the wine-cellars. He long ago tore up his letters from Pound, from Yeats, from Eliot, from Ford Madox Ford. He has probably lost his copy of Hemingway's first book, from Robert MacAlmon's Contact Press. There's still a copy of Mina Loy's *Lunar Baedecker* (sic), 1923, on the shelf, which he would never consider selling for the thousand dollars it's worth in 1983.

Bunting is a "quirkie bodie, capable o' making law no law at a'," in Galt's phrase. He is a catbird, and one must laugh with him—and at him—as he delights in doing himself. He insists he has no virtues that he can think of, and for an epitaph he would be happy with: **MINOR POET, NOT CONSPICUOUSLY DISHONEST.** Since I am nearly as much of a metrophobe as he is, we get along quite well. Basil these days looks a proper subject for the lens of Julia Margaret Cameron—in the mould of Alfred Lord Tennyson—, but he hates the Kensington/Chiswick world she represented. Much of what he takes for canon he learned by the age of 22. For 60 years that knowledge has sustained him in his arrogant (and modest) Modernism. I think you get him very wrong, however, if you take him to be the statue of Ozymandias and all that. What he is is a very complicated, alienated poet, with opinions strictly out there on their own. A few of us listen very hard when he gives utterance. He both likes giving utterance and he hates it. He is self-dismissive and self-satisfied. There is more than a touch of the "slovenly." He often says precisely the opposite of what he stands for. One can only drink to that. What I value most is his hard, sharp music, and his insistence that poetry is made by privateers for "unabashed boys and girls."

What follows is compiled to guide some of these young folk. Who are poets? Occasionally they are genuine craftsmen and women who work the language in astonishing ways. The others are, at best, merely *pompiers*, loud-mouths, sore-heads, creatures of cliques and coteries, the untalented, the hired minions of institutes, academies, universities. They are intellectualized tire-salesmen and motel-keepers. They are not, as they say, *for real*. There is codswallop and common sense in what follows. Laugh a little, learn a little, and take it as it comes. Squire Bunting says: "What the hell, it's all rubbish. Put it on a string and hang it up in the bathroom!"

## THE DIALOGUE

Along with 1983's longest day and the mysterious advent of actual sunshine on the center court at Wimbledon, Mr. Bunting has arrived in his venerable, rusty Daf motor car at Corn Close for his annual siesta-cum-fiesta. This features Tom Meyer as *chef de cuisine* and conversationist, serving up opinion, linguistics, joints of beef, pesto, Blue Wensleydale, curries, apple tarts, etc., for washing down with Theakston's bitter beer, the Wine Society's aged Rioja, and Hugel's Gewürztraminer. Tennis and the deracination of dandelion from the garden occupy my mind this week until evenings. And then it's time to open the Caledonian firewater and discuss the vagaries of poetry and the miseries of the times. Last night we did considerable damage to a bottle of Lagavulin malt whisky from the Island of Islay. The carton describes "the grandeur of Lagavulin." David Daiches's book uses the adjective "robust." Good whisky ought to produce good talk, and even the odd good thought. Basil got to grumbling about the infirmities of the aged. But, he's still driving a car at 83 (often at 83 mph); he's quicker in the head than most men in Northumberland or anywhere else. "I'm bloody useless these days," he says. "Well," says I, "we'll have to call you the Tarset Zombie." Eventually BB fell asleep while Jorge Bolet began to play Franz Liszt in a very grand manner. Then he was spared Earl Wild's breathtaking transcriptions of some of the Rachmaninoff songs. While he dozed, I got to thinking that we should devote some time this week to putting down on paper the poems and poets he would put into the fabled *Anthology* that he has spoken of compiling for many years now. Lest he never get around to the job, the basic information ought to be made available. (Some of it does exist on tape, in a reading BB has made for Newcastle University.) Back in 1977 when I asked Basil about the *Anthology,* he said this: "The plan was not to put in the best poets necessarily, or the best poems, but try and demonstrate from the English everybody knows—to try and show the principles on which poetry works. Right up to 1640 you can say that a poet wasn't a poet unless he was capable of playing a musical instrument and composing his poems to that. If you will read Wyatt and Sidney and Campion you'll get a good idea of poetry as song. But Sidney's slightly older contemporary, Spenser, invented a new thing which has given a complexion to English verse ever since, so one must have Spenser there also. Spenser made the words produce their own music, instead of depending on the musician to do it."

Since BB's master-list of poets (Homer, Ferdosi, Dante, Manucheri, Hafez, Aneirin, Heledd, Malherbe, Wyatt, Spenser, Sidney, Wordsworth) includes only four who wrote in English, this 1983 *Anthology* is wide-ranging indeed. It's too bad that it will ignore the oddities and eccentrics. If there were fifty poets under consideration, Mr. Lear would have a place. And of course, Basil's six-liner attributed to Samuel Butler, from "A Satire on the Players":

> You smock-fac'd lads, secure your gentle bums;
> For, full of lust and fury, see he comes!
> 'Tis bugg'ring Nokes, who damn'd unwieldly tarse
> Weeps, to be bury'd in his footman's arse.
> Unnatural sinner, lecher without sense,
> To leave kind whores, to dive in excrements!

Hot stuff for the early 18th century. Anyway, if we promise our learned friend all the apple tart he can eat—plus a bottle each of Talisker, Glenfiddich, Glenmorangie, Highland Park and Laphroaig—during our deliberations, I will put him to work and ask him simply to tell us what he thinks it is necessary for a writer or reader of poetry to know since the days of Herakleitos. However, today, June 21st, being the birthday of

Jean-Paul Sartre, we will spend the morning throwing up and then watch Gerulaitis at Wimbledon. Tomorrow is more auspicious: the birthday of Sir Henry Rider Haggard and the Opening of Parliament.

**JW:** *Before we begin making chronological lists, Basil, I think I should tell you that two intrepid scholars in the USA have suggested to us over the winter that there is credibility to the fact that you carried on a homosexual romance with Ezra Pound.*

**BB:** Good god, man! What will they think of next? Ezra would have been absolutely horrified. He was a bit of a prude in some ways. Nobody would have been offended with Jacob Epstein for keeping six mistresses had he not been an inch deep in dirt and dust.

**JW:** *It's always been hard to believe in the half-dozen bastards of various hues fathered by Walt Whitman between the Crescent City and the City of Brotherly Love . . . Anyway, one more diversion. Take a glance at a book-list that Edward Dahlberg prepared for his* Festschrift. *I had a London bibliographer check the holdings of the British Museum for availability of the texts. Two of the books did not seem to exist—ever.*

**BB:** Interesting, but pretty much a washout for me. I've only read two or three of them.

**JW:** *Me too. Ah, "there is hope for us all—if we only get good pitching," to quote the ancient baseball truism. That's precisely what we need, a list of poets who can play good old country hardball. So, where do we start?*

**BB:** Considering what is available to us, we must start with Homer, a Greek probably active in Asia Minor between the 8th and 7th centuries B.C. He may have actually written his works with the new alphabetic writing, one of the very earliest to do so. People of my generation tended to be *Odyssey* people, but I have always preferred the firm architecture of the *Iliad*, which is as solid as a play and not just wandering along like an adventure story. That's the main thing, the simple architecture. It is a young man's book; the *Odyssey* is a *nostos*, a late book of the Trojan return.

**41**

Turning from epic to lyric, there is Sappho. Read her in the Greek with a crib, that's the way. There is no other poet who has left such a single, definite mark as Sappho, all with one poem . . . Pindar—for those who can read him fluently in Greek.

My impression is that Catullus's translation of the Sappho may be better than the original. There is an education in comparing the two texts. Catullus may have done things a bit tighter. Catullus and Lucretius managed to do their own thing as well as one can possibly imagine. The lesson to be learned from some half dozen of Catullus's poems for poets now is their extreme directness.

Pound was very interested in the Late Greeks. Theocritus is the one everybody knows and there are some very nice things. But I wouldn't worry with him. The genre is very lady-like and drawing-room. I am very ignorant of them.

Obviously we cannot lay out an historical survey in a few pages. There are masses of things of much interest along the way. But what we want here are some of the poets I know and remember, whose work might be an aid to a writer learning the craft.

There is, for instance, the unique figure of Aneirin, in the Bythonic or Proto-Welsh tradition of 5th of 6th centuries A.D. The repetition of the formula, with variations, is a very important part of a poem. Often he utters only two or three words in mourning the men in the Battle of Catraeath, but these words are very telling. There's a prose translation by Jackson of Edinburgh, which must be read with the Welsh opposite. It's a hard task. It is something I am extremely glad to have come across, but not until my old age, alas.

Heledd is perhaps no more than a century later. She laments the people at a battle near Shrewsbury. She has two or three poems in which she scores by the repetition of slightly varying refrains. Devastating poems, if you have any imagination. Not the sort of poem that goes down well at the present time. Some say she never existed. But the poems do.

Stauell Gyndylan ys tywyll heno
heb dan heb wely
wylaf wers tawaf wedy

(Cynddylan's hall is dark tonight;
no fire, no bed.
I'll weep awhile and then be still.)

This is a small sample of Heledd from *An Introduction to Welsh Poetry (From the Beginning to the Sixteenth Century)*, by Gwyn Williams, Faber & Faber, London, 1953. From here you must go to big libraries. It's a terrible thing. I get old, I get lost. I know so little about these things. And yet, they are *important*. How astonishingly tied together those words are, the rhymes, the alliteration. You have to use every scrap of your face to speak Welsh.

**JW:** *Before we jump one or two more centuries, I have a feeling we need to say—yet one more time—what we're doing here. I am asking you for a list (including remote languages that barely exist in translation) of the Great Instructors, the ones you read to learn how to construct your poems. That's all. So we have not had, for instance, any of the* Greek Anthology, *or any Martial, or Propertius, or even of your admired Horace. I remember somewhere you were saying about* hats, *that the important things are to make a hat or to wear a hat. The maker needs instruction how to utilize his time and material with economy. The wearer wants a product that is attractive by its color and texture, and by its ability to keep out the rain or the sun or the cold. And to be of a style that is not necessarily outlandish. The hat is not an abstract noun or something you want to spend your life thinking about. You wear it or you don't. For those who thrive on aesthetic feelings, you read poems and listen to Mr. Scarlatti's sonatas and Mr. Grieg's lyric pieces, and you learn how to bake a decent loaf—these are crafted objects that make life a more complex and interesting experience to get on with. There is a place up Dentdale called Lea Yeat, "the gate to the clearing." A*

**43**

lea *is a place that has been cleared and, sometimes, cultivated. Its root seems to be tied with* lucere, *to shine. Most of us respond to the shapeliness of a field under light and our ears and eyes do the same thing when words and letters are assembled with the elegance of a dry-stone wall amidst the heathen limestone. You might just say a few words on what you expect the finest poems to yield before we go on. I hope you will remind people that a poem is not an exercise for the intellect.*

**BB:** It's what I always say: a poem is a series of sounds in the air, just as music. Other things can be included or loaded on to it, but the essential thing is just the *noise.* That's a little less easy to see when discussing epic poetry, as we mostly have been doing, because epic includes a story. Hel-edd is merely making a wailing noise. It conveys very little information.

**JW:** *Where do we go next?*

**BB:** Ferdosi, about 900 A.D. at the end of the Dark Ages, well before the Norman Conquest. He handles story in several different ways than Homer did in his epics and there is much to be learned if your interest is narrative. Also, he inserts lyric details in places, something Homer was chary of, if my memory serves. I would put him and Homer at the very top of the ability to write poetry; they both seem capable of almost anything at a moment's notice. Ferdosi can suddenly be unutterably simple and naive and baffle you by being so moving at the same time. Other times he is patterned, intricate, pretty-pretty like a Persian carpet, with no particular commitments, but equally astonishing. Obviously, you see I am moved by my memory of his work, but how to convey this to the reader? He'd have to learn Persian and see for himself. There is no adequate translation of *Shahnameh.*

Manucheri? He had no talent for epic at all, but almost everything else that poetry can do he does and it always compares with the best anywhere. He is direct as Catullus and Robert Burns—quite overwhelming. There are his pieces achieved by complex patterning. There are no comparisons in English, saving, perhaps, bits of early Swinburne. There is a poem about literature—the sort of Dunbar thing ("Where are the poets

**44**

of Yesteryear?"), in which there is a page of the names of the poets, a great sonorous roll of poetry. That is magnificent stuff. In his stanzaic poems he combines an extraordinary command of patterning (equal to that in the *Lindisfarne Gospels*) with perfect exactitude. The names of the flowers are absolutely correct, everything fits because of accuracy, not to fill out a form. And there is not one trace of Neo-Platonic Mysticism, all that bloody stuff that European Orientalists are always looking for. I don't believe he gave two hoots for God, ever. He was a good Mazanderani pagan. You can read him in Persian, with the help of Kazimirski's footnotes in Latin. How do you learn Persian? Sit down with the greatest book in the language and get yourself a proper dictionary. Eventually you know where you are.

Hafez, next, about 1300. He depends entirely on sound, there is little else. In the famous second poem of his *Divan*, in about 14 or 15 couplets, he is merely telling you that he won't be able to come to dinner. Tears come to ones eyes over such beauty. He is an extremist case. There are lots of translations made by people who think he was expounding good Sufi doctrine. I don't believe it a minute. Gertrude Bell's would be the best translations, but they're not good. The sound is sometimes there.

**JW:** *Since we're sticking to chronological order in our masters, the next on the list would be Dante.*

**BB:** What can you say, really? To begin with, he is very thoroughly organized, and this extreme organization is very terse. He had thought a great deal about language and poetry and he stated quite unambiguously in the *De Vulgari Eloquio* that what matters is the sound of the words—without that there isn't even poetry. He took great freedoms with the eleven-syllable line that he was using, and this fact is disguised by the grammarians who invent exceptions to all the supposed rules in order to fit Dante's practice. The combination of extremely terse and vivid language with a sonority which is always adapted to what is going on makes practically the whole of the *Commedia* (for the people who bother to read it in Italian) absolutely unforgettable. You'll remember more lines and passages of Dante than any other poet. His criticism is just as worth reading, if you're going to learn to write. No one has given such good advice. An enormous amount of later poetry—Italian, French, Spanish, English—stems directly from Dante, or indirectly, via Petrarch for instance.

What would be the next one in time. Wyatt learned to write lyric poetry in Italian to his own accompaniment on the lute, which is what the Italian poets were used to doing. Naturally, he made use of the devices of song-writers and composers of his day. This has puzzled some of his successors, because after Wyatt's time people started compiling prosodies and expected everything to be put regular in verse, whereas the musicians had been used to using much syncopation, which, of course, did not agree with the stomp-and-bump of the prosodists—many of who still haven't learned. All Wyatt's editors until well into this century thought they could write better poetry than Wyatt and altered him accordingly. Notably, Sir Arthur Quiller-Couch in the *Oxford Book of English Verse*. Wyatt's poetry is practically all for singing. When he is supposedly mis-translating some of the Italians, he is merely making them singable in English.

Malherbe, three-quarters of a century after Wyatt, was still writing to be sung. He complained to his friend Racan that he had been handicapped all his life because he had never been taught to finger the lute. He paid immense attention to the texture of his verse, so that he could make a perfectly smooth stanza out of the ordinary spoken syntax of French. He has fallen out of fashion because he spent a lot of time writing eulogies of kings and statesmen—a fashion which no longer exists—but the texture of the work is always superb.

**JW:** *I don't recall ever hearing any Malherbe. Can you find a few passages?*

**BB:** (*Scanning a volume from the shelf, turning the pages.*) Bugger! This old brain of mine can't seem to find anything except what I don't want. I

46

may have to try to recite some from memory. (*And he does.*) Damn! Blast! I can't even find the ode about the young girl which has such surprisingly beautiful lines ... (*And then Bunting reads two stanzas from a "Consolation," remarkable in their poise and their ease.*) Must have taken him weeks to achieve that simplicity. I am told that in the 1970s the French again began studying Malherbe like mad.

**JW:** *We seem to have chosen one of the hottest days in Northumberland in years* (the interview is continuing at Greystead Cottage, Tarset, in the North Tyne Valley on July 13th) *to reflect on poetry.*

**BB:** We have. Of course, if you want to think about hot summers, you have to go back to 1911. That was hot! But, before I decay away entirely, let's get on. Spenser? And Sidney? What can I say about these fellows? They were particularly interested in the sound of English words. Sidney spent a great deal of time investigating quantity in verse instead of stress. Spenser tried his hand at it, but he was interested in so many aspects of versification that he let it drop. He wrote "The Shepherd's Calendar" to show the great variety of English versification, so that poets, for several generations after, could dip into Spenser and find what they wanted to imitate. *The Fairie Queene* doesn't exhaust all his possibilities of meters, always he is discovering and making use of the possibilities of the sound of the language. Almost anybody after Spenser is to some extent indebted to him, either directly or second-hand.

I don't think people would normally take Milton to be Spenserian, but Milton was predominantly influenced by Fairfax, who was deeply influenced by Spenser. To the poets of a generation and a half after him, Spenser was just as much of the innovator as Ezra Pound has been for the poets of this century. It's not only the texture which is so interesting. He planned his poems in such surprising ways, no two alike. Poems such as the "Four Hymns" or "Mother Hubbard's Tale" are among the first of their kind, and still among the best of their kind. And the great sequence, which begins with a large number of rather tranquil and expectable sonnets, leading unexpectedly to a quarrel which leaves the reader guessing, until the poet goes on suddenly into the "Epithalamion" to fill in the gap as you will—the greatest processional hymn that I know!

**JW:** *I know that you're now going to jump two centuries (a little over) to a poet from Cockermouth in Cumbria named William Wordsworth.*

**BB:** Late Milton is worth taking note of. It's a terribly literary affair, but the subject matter makes it tolerable. "Samson" and great chunks of *Paradise Lost*... I can't think of anybody else. Ezra Pound would have put in Pope. He liked that kind of flowing mellifluence. I don't know. He liked Pope and didn't like Tennyson. Curious.

As for Wordsworth, the value of him as a poet (as opposed to the "mystic" and "pantheist") is complicated by the fact that most of the commentators cannot speak his language. They speak "Kensington" and do not think of Wordsworth as musical. In fact, he is very musical. He wrote in very plain language, usually with very plain syntax, and made it musical and forceful all at once. That's there. What's never mentioned is his extreme narrative skill, greater than any other poet in English save Chaucer, perhaps. Secondly, they overlook his humour. Very comic stuff, an early kind of humour that again reminds one of Chaucer. "The Idiot Boy" is very funny; so is "The Waggoner." And in short poems too: "Goody Blake" is very funny. I get roars of laughter when I read it, and I'm not guying it. Above all, narrative skill is what a poet today could learn from Wordsworth.

The fact is that you don't have to have far-fetched, bloody-poetical words in order to have beauty of sound. There's no need to candy things up as Keats did, as Tennyson did, it only gets in the way. Wordsworth knew that sugar-candy is not a good diet. Prettiness is often a trap. A great deal of all this finally comes down to having read the literature, of knowing what the words can do and have done—by your *reading,* not by looking words up in the philologist's dictionary. Then you handle words with some notion of the overtones they carry. To Shakespeare a girl was a girl. Several centuries earlier a girl was a young man. Aye, it's important to know these things.

**JW:** *Elsewhere you've said the basic advice is make them learn English grammar—especially syntax.*

**BB:** The most splendid place to find good syntax is in Jonathan Swift. For instance, *A Tale of a Tub.* Yeats noticed that Wordsworth's plain vocabulary was incomplete without a plain syntax. Carlos Williams is important for his beautiful, clear syntax.

**JW:** *I remember that Swift said: All you have to do is get the right word in the proper place.*

**BB:** Aye, that's good. It begs two questions. One thinks of Joyce or Flaubert spending weeks over a single comma, over one preposition.

I sometimes recommend a non-poet to aspiring writers as someone who can teach them about putting things together: and that is Charles Darwin. But I should have said about Wordsworth that occasionally his stress on "thing" is remarkable. Any competent writer must know the importance of *things.* The moment you leave off into abstract words you lose touch, with the reader and the music and the world. So stay away from Plato.

**JW:** *I just ran into the word* Musaphobia, *which seems to mean either a fear of mice or a fear of poems. One has known mature adults who leap on tables or throw up their skirts when either a wee beastie or a wee poem enters their house. I would say that there is a general epidemic of Musaphobia abroad in the year 1983.*

**BB:** The times are squalid. They always were. It is a poet's duty to hold the line.

**JW:** *And hold his Glenfiddich. Cheers, Basil. Your health!*

(Conjunctions 5, *edited by Bradford Morrow, New York, 1983)*

# THE HARDY BOYS GO TO WORK
# AT CARMEN SUTRA'S BOOKSTORE

Just before Marc Schleifer wrote, asking for a comment on Henry Miller, I was reading the March issue of *Commentary* in the Monterey library. In it there is a superb piece by Paul Goodman on "Pornography, Art & Censorship." For me, he calls all the shots, one after another.

For instance, he considers it the Supreme Court's duty not to corrupt the youth, "to call *not* obscene whatever tends to joy, love, and liveliness, including the stirring of lustful impulses and thoughts." The latter mildly obfuscated phrase means simply a desire to masturbate or copulate. So, what's wrong with that? asks Goodman. "In our culture an artist is expected to move the reader; he is supposed to move him to tears, to laughter, to indignation, compassion, even to hatred; but he may not move him to have an erection or to mockery of public figures making spectacles of themselves. Why not? . . . 'Dwight Eisenhower at Columbia' is a title to rouse an Aristophanes . . ." Why not have some decent sex in the culture, instead of all the schlock? Less J. Edgar Hoover and more Henry Miller? There is, after all, a very moving limerick on the difficulty of selling sex commercially:

the team of Tom and Louise
do an act in the nude on their knees;
they crawl down the aisle
while fucking dog-style,
and the orchestra plays Kilmer's "Trees"

I certainly contend that the copy of Pierre Louys' *Aphrodite* (Modern Library edition) behind all the RCA Victor red-seal albums of Toscanini's Beethoven was more salubrious to my adolescence than the official reading imposed by secondary education. Can you imagine having to read Sir James Barrie's *The Little Minister* at age 15? I had to—and *Lorna Doone* too. But, thank god for *Time* magazine. It so insulted and vilified Miller's *The Air-Conditioned Nightmare* (1945) that I soon had, in addition, most of his *banned* books—hidden back of the Sibelius symphonies conducted by Koussevitsky. So what's wrong with it? They helped make life endurable, sanguine, and a mite lubricious. They swung, like W. C. Fields' breakfast: half a glass of fresh orange juice and four double-martinis. He lived a long time.

Now that I am writing this in California, on the northern edge of the Big Sur, Miller is gone from Partington Ridge—likely for good. He's in Hamburg, Germany, writing his first play (at 71). There are, meanwhile, many rumors that American editions of the *Tropics* are soon forthcoming. Only very sick people will be offended by them. He likes what he likes, that's all: sex, steak (and sex after steak), astrology (and sex after astrology) . . . "The more you come, the more you can," to quote further wisdom from Paul Goodman. Do you not agree with Anatole France that chastity is the most bizarre of sexual perversions? Twenty sexual athletes could no more run the Miller One-Man Endurance Course than they could negotiate a series of the good Marquis de Sade's *tableaux* and come back for more. However, a little lumpen-type Bud-drinker's bragging never hurt anybody. Remember that Priapus liked to do it on volcanic sand beaches well before the invention of KY jelly.

I don't have my Miller collection at hand, but the books "not for import into the British Isles and the United States of America" would include: *Tropic of Cancer*, *Tropic of Capricorn*, *Black Spring*, *Max & The White Phagocytes*, *The World of Sex*, *Sexus* and *Nexus* (parts I and II of *The Rosy Crucifixion*), and *Quiet Days in Clichy*. I.e., the essential Henry Miller, excepting *The Colossus of Maroussi*. Anyone, exercising the slightest wit and imagination, can secure all this good stuff from friends abroad, in Europe or Japan.

The painter Ephraim Doner, *grand maître* of Carmel Highlands, tells this anecdote about his friend Henry Miller, who had just returned from a trip to France. The customs official in New York City asked his name. He replied, "Henry Miller." "Henry Miller?—not the writer?" "No, Henry Miller, the plumber." "Gee, that's too bad. Me and Al, the guy over at the desk there, we have a whole bunch of books by a guy named Henry Miller. We keep hoping to meet him coming through here, so we can ask him to autograph them."

*(Unpublished, 1961)*

# "I DON'T CARE IF I NEVER GET BACK": A SPLASH WITH JAMES MCGARRELL IN MAX BECKMANN'S (NOT PIERRE BONNARD'S) BATHTUB

These shambolic days, with the Republic flooded with Vapidians, Mammonites, Floridians, and the Certifiably Brain-Dead Boring, my interest in hot artists and price-tag art has dwindled. Product and career have wiped out vision and character.

But I was delighted to be asked to write some words about James McGarrell. We meet occasionally over the years (Umbria, Cumbria, Indiana, Champaign/Urbana—and even in places that don't rhyme like New York and La Napoule). The first time was a summer evening in 1952 at *Luthgen's*, a dance club in a black neighborhood of New Orleans. I was on army furlough. Jim was there with the redoubtable and inimitable jazz historian and musician, Bill Russell, to hear George Lewis and one of his finest bands: Alcide "Slow Drag" Pavageau, Lawrence Marrero, Jim Robinson, Joe Watkins, Alton Purnell, Percy Humphrey—the names are still fresh in the mind. I hitch-hiked 550 miles to the Crescent City to hear these men play. (Jim, by the way, had hitched some 830 from Indiana for this pleasure.) And now, 37 years later, I just drove 750 miles to St. Louis to talk to Jim McGarrell. I might do the same to see high art by R. B. Kitaj, Jess, or Diebenkorn; low art by Edgar Tolson, Bill Traylor, or Thornton Dial—the list is very short.

James McGarrell is a poised, deliberate, dapper cousin of the North

American Bison. He has always looked like Henri Matisse's grandson. He has been married to the poet Ann McGarrell for 35 of his 59 years, and a son Andrew and a daughter Flora Raven are the off-spring of this union. He lives quietly, courtesy of a hard-working life devoted to painting and exemplary teaching. He drives a Honda Civic with 120,000 miles on it.

His myriad brushes are neatly sorted and so are his boxes and boxes of Holbein oil pastels. He is a thoughtful host. When you stay in his studio the air-conditioning works, there is a bar of excellent soap, the Neutragena shampoo and conditioner are new. There is decent white wine in the fridge, the towels are fresh and there is an extra roll of toilet paper. Plenty of books on Vermeer and Veronese and Van Gogh; videotapes of Pound, W. C. Williams, and Wallace Stevens; audiocassettes of Auden and Basil Bunting. He will even order you a Cardinals game from cable-tv, and go out and get the Popeye fried chicken, red beans, rice, and biscuits to complement it. His art, sited in the domain of quite complex pleasure, dovetails nicely with a life as comfortable as Matisse's famous armchair. McGarrell remarks: "I noticed early on that the French artists' studios I saw in picture books looked like living rooms. Studios of American artists looked like garages."

One senses mild unrest when McGarrell is asked to palaver. Cézanne would say to art bores: "Ok, boys, let's cut the crap, let's all get down to work. *Travaillons!*" Since I had come to town to ask the kind of questions dumb poets always ask, he endured the grilling with both detachment and amusement. He talked of "the studio" constantly. In three days of conversation, never one moan about those Four Horsemen of MacPainting: *Glitz, Chic, Hype & Schlock*, who permeate art talk these days like the ads for incontinence-control on tv. McGarrell has exhibited widely (with Frumkin/Adams in New York, Struve in Chicago, Claude-Bernard in Paris, Roncaglia in Rome, Gian Ferrari in Milan), is in many collections, makes a "decent" living. To get the artist commenting about the work itself, we sat and looked through a series of current monotypes he's been working over with oil pastel, and through a batch of slides of some of the big paintings of the past few years. Here are remarks by McGarrell I found particularly illuminating:

I didn't start painting till I was 20, that was in the basement of the family home in Indianapolis. Later, when I became an art student, the first teachers who stroked and stimulated me were Alton Pickens, Jack Levine, George Rickey, and Henry Varnum Poor.

What I call pictorial invention is nothing but memory, recombined and sprung into life by making colored marks. Although I don't paint directly from nature or drawings or photographs, I would never paint anything I hadn't seen, or had a possibility of seeing. These pictures are works of the imagination, not fantasy.

It was about 1970 when I decided that every figure in my paintings must be performing some act, even one as passive as reading or drinking a cup of contemplative coffee. They couldn't just be there posing for the viewer.

You've just mentioned to me that a central tenet of Charles Olson's was: **ONE LOVES ONLY FORM!** To which I would want to say: *maybe.* For we have also just heard Basil Bunting say that meaning is important in poetry but music (form?) is indispensable. A lot of poetry "means" very little. Some passages in my paintings are clearly legible as images of particular objects or events, some are only suggestive, and others are not readable at all (or can be read as several wildly different kinds of things). Behind everything, though, is a ground beat of old-fashioned, formal, pictorial geometry.

Somebody once said my subjects could be divided up into food, music, and sex. Meat is very interesting to paint, when you think what meat is.

Those of us who paint figuratively and perhaps also those who respond to our work sometimes need reminding that paintings are *made* objects. They are constructed, they are invented, they are fiction, they are synthetic. No matter how referential, they are not reflections of something else; they don't grow naturally, they are a willed something. The power of the thing they are may be a derived power, but never a borrowed one, for it cannot be given back, and it refuses testing by its original source.

You ask how I view my position in the frantic big-money international art world. I know I'm doing important stuff that a number of people take seriously, but I don't kid myself that the art establishment sees it as having the stature of any number of artists I consider less than peers. If I am right that my work is underrated, that's probably the result of several circumstances —that I've never been part of a broad influential movement; that my dealers have never been the trendy ones; or, maybe most of all, that I've chosen to live and teach in midwestern universities and Europe, while only my paintings are on view in Manhattan and the West Coast. One of the good things about this removal is that I don't stew or bristle because my nose is being constantly rubbed in the celebrity of negligible artists I wouldn't find interesting even as students.

My immodest hope is that I might one day be seen as one of those otherwise significant painters who worked in provincial places with some recognition but little influence on the contemporary mainstream. I'm vain enough to say I'm thinking of artists like Eakins, Ensor, and Piero; and, more recently, Edwin Dickinson or C. S. Price. They were not the Michelangelos, Caravaggios, or Picassos, who changed the whole visual map in their lifetimes, but I'd rather join their ranks than those of the Bougereaux and Warhols, more social phenomena than artists and more interesting on the score of facile contemporary celebrity than for inventive substance.

That night in Jim's studio I happened across this passage from Gilles Aillaud's book on Vermeer: "It was certainly no chance that the extraordinary ability Vermeer possessed simply passed unnoticed by his contemporaries—causing no stir, no scandal, invisible, as if he simply belonged to another century, another species altogether."

Since I long ago took to heart some excellent advice by Rainer Maria Rilke ("Read as few works of criticism or aesthetics as possible."), I know very well there are ways of gaining insight into works of art and artists themselves without resorting to *artspeak* and *bafflegab*. While McGarrell's answers to naming the ten best proctologists practicing in the Ozarks, or naming the ten outstanding tuba players along the length of Arkansas River, might be the same as yours or mine, other information is cogent.

Ten Favorite Jazz Musicians: "Johnny Dodds has to be Number One. King Oliver, Jimmy Noone, Jelly Roll Morton, Louis Armstrong, Ben Webster, Charlie Parker, Billie Holiday, Bunk Johnson, Emile Barnes, Lester Young, George Lewis. Coleman Hawkins, Fats Waller—that's 14, I can't just name ten. Wish I could think of a white one."

Ten Favorite Restaurants That Spring To Mind: "First, two obvious ones, *Arthur Bryant's* in Kansas City for barbecued pork ribs, and *La Pyramide* (1965) in Vienne; we ate there when Fernand Point was still alive ... *M. Brun*, in Marseilles, for spicy, piquant hors d'oeuvres ... *Da Mencuccio* in Trestina in Umbria—in your company, or that of Bill Bailey's family, or Jack and Sondra Beal—for the tortellini alla panna, the bruschetta, and the chocolate ice cream ... the spaccio *Cantarelli* at Samboseto ... Chicago: *Pizzeria Uno* and *Avanzare*—a wild mushroom dish with slices and garnishes of things ... St. Louis: *Richard Perry's Restaurant* at the *Hotel Majestic* downtown. He cooks 'Missouri' with a *nouvelle* attack ... In New York City I like the dairy restaurants downtown; *Rappaport's* is excellent ... So many in Paris: *Miraville* on the *rive gauche* ... the *Cantina Laredo* in Dallas ... *Galatoire's* in New Orleans, still unpretentious and good."

Ten Favorite Sports Figures: "Elgin Baylor, Jimmy Rayl, Frank Robinson, Sugar Ray Robinson, Roy Campanella, Larry Bird, Willie Mays, Ilie Nastase, Archie Moore, and Ozzie Smith. These are certainly not all "greatest" but ones I have watched with great pleasure. Anyway, a few *are* white."

One afternoon McGarrell and I walked around in the *St. Louis Museum of Art*. Again, I asked him for specific responses to work he felt strongly about:

Max Beckmann . . . Visceral, sensuous, not geometric; information carried in the memory, re-presented, not represented . . . the roughness of the painting attack, putting it down, scraping it off, putting it down and moving it around . . . I got my bathtubs from Beckmann, not from Bonnard . . . the inclusive range of his subjects; the French were getting rid of things while he filled his canvases with impossibly particular objects.

Of living abstract artists, I don't know anybody doing better work than Howard Hodgkin.

Matisse, "Bathers With a Turtle," what a very tough painting for 1908.

That late Titian, the paint, the brush moving across . . .

Hans Holbein the Younger, "Mary Lady Guildford," real dynamite, that lapis blue background, the green tendril against blue—wonderful tonalities.

The Butchering Scenes, Tomb of Prince Mentuemhat (730–525 B.C.), Egypt, Asasif Valley—look at the speed of those contour lines, and its carved stone.

So, let's leave Jim McGarrell busy making monotypes in the studio. One ear is tuned to the Cardinals' broadcast from Busch Stadium. Reasons for cheer: Vince Coleman and Jose Oquendo each singled twice, walked, stole a base, and scored twice in the second game against the Braves. Still, the boys are only playing .530 ball and there are only six weeks until October. Shift to NPR, listen to one of Fauré's piano quintets, put a filet on the grill, and open up the Rubesco Torgiano. *Bon soir*, Monsieur McGarrell!

*(From* The Art of James McGarrell, *Frances Wolfson Art Gallery,
Miami-Dade Community College, Miami, Florida, 1990)*

# ROBERT DUNCAN (1919-1988)

Let's leave the Great Poet stuff well alone! For us deprived and isolated Americans, was he the Apollinaire *de nos jours*? The Satie? The Dante? The Goethe? We over-estimate ourselves, we democratic poets with so little background power of any kind. Robert Duncan was as good a *phantaste* and romancer as Gabriel Fauré—there is nothing wrong with that, though perhaps only 59 persons in the world knew to listen for his angelic whirrings.

Duncan was born in California. He enjoyed being a sage and a mage. He could out-talk R. Buckminster Fuller and the Wicked Witch of the West put together. Even Samuel Taylor Coleridge might have found himself gasping for air and being swept away by this river of sacred conversation. It needs very much to be said that Duncan was the absolute master of the campy imagination. Otherwise, the academic and boring straight-arrows will suddenly try to claim him for their own and startle us with the revelation that Mr. Lowell was not the only Robert around. I have been around long enough to remember what Charles Olson once wrote (granted, it was early on) in the margins of my copy of Duncan's "An African Elegy": "Stay away from fairies and Platonists!" Oy yoy yoy! Of Mr. Olson, Mr. Ezra Pound once declared: "Stay away from kikes and

Olson!" We get a lot of muck from our very best poets. Their tongues are reet glibbery.

Another of the things that Robert Duncan was: the bard of gay domesticity. Most of our poets are company men (Corn-Belt Metaphysicals from Iowa; Ivy-League Late-Bloomers; Bible-Belt Preachers from Shitsplat, South Carolina; and California Stoned-Age Toughs), and it's hard to think of anyone further away from all that drek than Robert Duncan. When I visited him in 1954 in San Francisco, he was the first person I knew with *The Lord of the Rings* high on the shelves. He loved the Edith Sitwell of "Facade." He loved Lotte Lenya's singing of the Berlin and New York theatre songs of Kurt Weill. He loved George Macdonald's *At the Back of the North Wind*. And *Lilith*. He was the first person among my friends to recognize the special genius of the Scots poet, Ian Hamilton Finlay. He had a beautiful Burmese cat named Pumpkin, whom I had the pleasure of taking care of when RD went off to Mallorca. We shared tastes on the margins of American culture: Randolph Bourne, Dahlberg, Zukofsky, Bruce Goff, Enid Foster, and, of course, Jess Collins, the astonishing painter who was central to RD's life for over 37 years. This is what I mean by the powerful domesticity of Robert Duncan's being. Early on Jess's paintings and collages had not seemed all that compelling. Then one day in the 1960s his work became absolutely primary—in some magical way the doing of both Jess and his extraordinary partner.

I feel badly that I had hardly seen the man for 20 years. I sympathize completely with Basil Bunting, when he said on hearing of the death of Louis Zukofsky: "You know, I can barely remember what I felt and who he was." (A telephone call from San Francisco intervenes at this precise moment: Ronald Johnson, one of our finest poets, whom so very few know, saying, "The thing is, despite three years of the most battering illness, Robert at the end was so strong and so sweet.")

One of Duncan's sayings is so true that I often think I would like to see it written by a sky-writer in the morning light over the Nantahala Mountains to the west of here: "**RESPONSIBILITY IS TO KEEP THE ABILITY TO RE-**

**SPOND.**'' Of the great 20th century anarchist/pacifist, libertarian traditions in American letters—we include Henry Miller and Kenneth Patchen and Paul Goodman and Kenneth Rexroth and Brother Antoninus and Thomas Merton—, Robert Duncan was nearly the last representative.

For the illustrations to his book *Letters,* Duncan made five drawings of his "Ideal Reader." She was a lady much like his beloved Beatrix Potter, plump and matronly in a big sun hat. Her responsibilities were to those of husbandry and the domestic: to sing and read, to water the garden, to brew the tea, to be nice to the cat.

*(* The Independent, *London, February 9, 1988)*

# THE ADVENTURES OF
# JAMES RICHARD BROUGHTON;
# OR, SPLASHING IN THE
# POETRY PUDDLE, TRYING TO
# KEEP GOD AMUSED

### 1.

Some readers may perhaps wish to heed the advice that the old song offered to the Damsel-in-Distress: "Run for the roundhouse, Nellie, the brakeman can't corner you there . . ." The point being, Mr. James Richard Broughton (aka Sunny Jim, aka Big Joy, aka Sister Sermoneta of the Sisters of Perpetual Indulgence, aka The Modesto Catbird) at full cry, as he is here in this New & Selected Poems, well, he's just about the rarest, queerest bird you ever heard boogie in the orphic barnyard. Mr. Broughton's elations are much too serious and much too joyous to be left to certifiably poem-dead criticasters to elucidate, so another erotomaniacal maker of frivolities was asked to praise his art. I accepted with pleasure. As was suggested long ago by the Reverend Robert Herrick (1591–1674), Vicar of Dean Prior, Devonshire: "Gather ye Rose-buds and Butt-holes while ye may!"

We may not know for sure that Ravel was *comme ça* (still, *we* know—it's the scholars, poor things, who don't know). Broughton leaves not the slightest doubt, even T. Danforth Quayle would know. Ever since his Angel woke him from sleep at the age of three, told him he would always be a poet, told him not to fear being alone, not to fear being laughed at, he's been singing those goatsongs and getting to the true Bottom of Things.

From Ga-Ga to Gay-Gay over half a century, doing that Lingam-Gambol! Every poem, a hymn to Priapus in his exceedingly comfortable logaoedic meter consisting of a catalectic Glyconic and a Pherecratean. Rootin'-tootin' broughton-spoutin' pricksongs, O Friends and Neighbors! Like I say, some will want to develop a migraine and go read the Gideon Bible or Robert Lowell. Why don't the rest of us just strip off and jump in the hot tub? Walt's over in the corner talking to Arty Rainbow and Pauline Verlaine, who has just this second quoted Victor Hugo: "Laughter is the soap of the gods."

Almost as noble as James Broughton's willingness to stand there naked as a jaybird, standing by its raucous word, is his willingness to use babytalk, prattle, doo-doo, goo-goo, and loony-camp lingo when called upon to do so. A lot of it works outrageously well. He reminds me of Jacques Tati playing tennis in *Les Vacances de Monsieur Hulot*. One imagines this bizarre figure coming onto the center court at Wimbledon to contest the formidable Boris "Boom Boom" Becker. He wears ancient tweeds, a floppy hat, smokes a pipe, carries a stone-age racket. Herr Becker serves and a fierce backhand drive to the baseline by Hulot leaves Boris standing there bug-eyed and flat-footed. *Touché*!

## 2.

Every poet has a *Jardin des Muses et des Herbes*. Every poet is influenced by absolutely everything and everybody of interest, else, why bother? However, go sniffing in James' garden and you will catch a whiff of:

> Mother Goose & Father Gander
> Mr. Edward Lear
> Walter "Snowbeard" Whitman
> Billy Blake
> Wystan Auden
> Arcangelo Corelli

Robert Duncan

Edith Sitwell

J. S. "Jazzbo" Bach

Igor Stravinsky

Jhan-Cock-Toe

Willie Yeats

e.e. cummings

Jim Joyce

Gert Rude-Stein

Ronald Firbank

Joe Brainard

Carl Jung

Vachel Lindsay

Jack Spicer

Franny Poulenc

Stevie Smith

Buster Keaton

Erik Satie

Wm Shake-It-But-Don't-Break-It

Sorrel

All-Spice

Elecampane

Mandragora

True & False Unicorn

Fenugreek

Ramp

Amanita Phalloides

## 3.

**ELEVEN QUOTATIONS TO THINK ABOUT AS YOU READ BROUGHTON:**

Nothing is true, everything is permitted.

*Hassan I Sabbah*

He is wholly herself when she plays with himself.

*Michael Amerlan*

At bottom, poetry, like all art, is inextricably bound up with giving pleasure, and if a poet loses his pleasure-seeking audience he has lost the only audience worth having, for which the dutiful mob that signs on every September is no substitute.

*Philip Larkin*

A key word in Franz Kline's vocabulary, which he used often (and which became a key word for me listening to him), is the word *delight* . . . he wanted to give it in his paintings as he wanted to give it in his life . . .

*Aaron Siskind*

Man outside the polis is either a beast or a god.

*Aristotle*

I'm not just a human being, I'm a piece of meat!

*Belial B. Behemoth*

At bottom, each person only understands his own love, and every other is foreign and unintelligible to him, if not repugnant. Here, too, only an understanding of the right to equal freedom, the tolerance of different lifestyles as the last and highest result of civilization, can have a beneficial effect.

*John Henry MacKay*

Chaste makes waste.

*Old Libertarian Saw*

It gets worse. In the upcoming film, Batman, sans Robin, is even given a heterosexual love interest! This is a crime worthy of the interest of the FBI. It is my hope that whoever the unlucky female is, that she does no better than the dogged Lois Lane, who has yet to pull the pants off Superman. And, after the last het kiss in the movie, I hope Batman goes to bed alone and beats off, dreaming of the long-gone Robin's firm young thighs.

*John Mitzel*

Read as few works of criticism or aesthetics as possible.

*Rainer Maria Rilke*

Peter Rose . . . is that a person or a sentence?

*The Apocryphal Oscar Wilde, commenting on
the Baseball Scandals of 1989*

## 4.

### WHERE I THINK BIG JOY IS AT HIS VERY BEST:

Two characters who make frequent appearances in James Broughton's poems are our friends, the *Puer Eternus* and the still-sinning *Pater Senex*. In the early poems the domain is often that of childhood. The forms are similar to nursery rhymes and the polished nonsense of Lear and Carroll. There is much in *Musical Chairs* and in *An Almanac For Amorists* that will delight anyone looking for formal elegance and a very exact vocabulary, one that holds lots of surprises and few terrors (*furfuraceous* and *pantophagous* will send you to James' favorite book, *Webster's Unabridged Dictionary*, 2nd edition). A few choice examples:

> I don't like his looks and he don't like me,
> but I'm a cowboy now and so is he.
> So I'm gonna get my gun and go shoot Jesus,
> I'm gonna shoot Jesus before he shoots me.
> *from "The Heir of the Parson"*

I'm a lightfoot buckaroo on a beehop pace
and Delicate Crazy is my hometown.
*from "The Clever Troubadour of Amoret County"*

She was my honey baby, she sure was my delight
    with her beautiful beady black eyes.
I met her in Modesto in the middle of the night
    when the old hotel burned down.
*from "The Girl With The Beady Black Eyes"*

Love so they tell me, love so I hear,
love waves the trumpet and butters the tree.
*from "Loony Tom's Song"*

Middle period Broughton fills us with the realization that into every life
a little Zen must fall. James spent a lot of time in Sausalito on Alan Watts'
houseboat, where there was always some very antic company: Piro
Caro, Zev, Jean Varda, Kermit Sheets, Daddy Waxwrath now and again.

I heard in the shell
    the throb of each cell
from flower and rock and feather.
    But loudest of all
    rang the quiet call
of Yes and No singing together.
*from "I Heard in the Shell"*

I don't know what the left is doing,
said the Right Hand,
but it looks fascinating.
*from* High Kukus

He became, he said, "a hometown swami who can't keep his month
shut." Then, the arrival of the cinematographer and artist, Joel Singer,

**67**

between Mr. Broughton's sheets and across the breakfast dishes, when the latter was 61, produced a new poet, an evangelist of élan vital, a colporteur of cosmic, erotic yawp:

> Nipples and cocks
> nipples and cocks
> Nothing tickles the palate like
> nipples and cocks

Out poured a torrent of paeans, hymns, invocations, ditzy-rams, and epicurean imperatives to get it on and get off often as you can. He surmises that "the soul resides in the genitals." There is a remarkable eucharistic litany called "Have The God," which concludes:

> I swallow the god in my mouth
>
> I sanctify in my throat
> am sanctified into my guts
>
> I have the god I have the god
> I have the god in my mouth

That's as wide open as Blake's "Glad Day" or any pronouncement in Whitman, but still very much J. Broughton. Calloo, callay, he chortles in his joy.

Three score and fifteen have not brought him low, though he teases us and himself with intimations of mortality: "I excel in doodle dawdle and drowse." "I no longer need to be smartass or do the right thing. I don't understand the world and never expect to . . . once I preferred to make cleverer things than turds, but now it doesn't matter, I have abandoned ambition and boredom for metaphysical questions." Some of his recent poems are as good as any he has written.

> Have you ever tried to
> take the world in your arms?
> It resists being snuggled.

Out all day setting fires
under crotches
that refuse to burn.
    *from "Defective Wiring"*

How often do you think about Death?
Death thinks about you all the time
Death is fatally in love with you and me
and his lust is known to be relentless
    *from "Thinking About Death"*

Enough snippets. You don't need a hired guide to get you into James Broughton's poetic underworld. It is all as plain as the noses on Janus's faces. The Man from Modesto (or Delicate Crazy, Amoret County, California, USA, whichever you prefer) is one distinguished hombre. *Special Deliveries* belongs on a top shelf in your library where some of the other names on the spines would be Duncan, Spicer, Rexroth, Patchen, Whalen, Merton, Cunningham, Laughlin, and Everson.

# 5.

I met James Broughton in San Francisco in 1955 and so have had the pleasure of his company, his poems, his films, and his letters for 35 years. I remember suppers and parties in Aspen, Mill Valley, Big Sur, Winston-Salem, and here in Dentdale. The Unbuttoned One is invariably sage, funny, polite, and friendly—a combination not often come by these days. Back in March, Tom Meyer and I went over to Port Townsend from Seattle to see the new place that James and Joel Singer have settled into. Nice and private, tucked away in the forest out past the old army fortifications. Poets seem among the last persons who work at making living an art instead of making money an obsessive curse.

You would expect good letters from such a felicitous writer: ". . . Wish you & Tom were still here. Rhododendrons are abloom and columbine too. The hot tub in moonlight is a special pleasure. We are considering naming our "estate" Zemmery Ridd which, surely you have not forgotten, is where the Oblong Oysters grow, near the great Gramboolian plain."

A more recent letter, written on Gay Liberation Day, June 25th, included a poem:

> Lord Nose, my dear one,
> what's to become of us?
> And all the other beauties of this world?
> Shall we just go on as we always have, mucking and fucking,
> mewling and pewling, hahaing and boohooing?
> Today it's for prancing and glancing and the old huzza!

And he added a postscript: "My films are off to the Moscow Film Festival: they requested sex & nudity! Glasnost indeed."

And so let us leave Sister Sermoneta and Cocky St. Jock (aka Joel Singer) entertaining their friends Sister Alice-Falice and Sister Boom Boom ("Nun of the Above"), mixing piss and vinegar, singing away in the hot tub in the wood where the Bong Tree grows, under the hills of the Chankly Bore. They'll be having some delicious crumbobblious cutlets for supper washed down with a jereboam of kickapoo joyjuice. Let the good times roll!

COCKADOODLEDOO, crowed the cockerel! COCK'LL DO ... COCK'LL DO JUST FINE, cried the poet!

*(Unpublished, rejected Introduction to* Special Deliveries
*[New and Selected Poems], by James Broughton,*
*Broken Moon Press, Seattle, WA, 1989)*

**70**

# A GARLAND FOR IAN GARDNER,

## SUBTITLED:

## HOUSES WELL STORED WITH

## TENDER EXOTICKS AND

## THE PARTERRS WITH SIMPLES

*F*ANFARE!

"Things aint never been the same since them three men went round the world."

"The Things we take for granted do not take Us so."

"*ACHTUNG! ACHTUNG! DING! DING!*"—which might be a quote from Ludwig Wittgenstein but is more likely Christian Morgenstern. *Bitte sehr*, there's biota there.

After that Handelian flourish, as played by Norman Hunter and the *Bradford City Knee-Biter Silver Band*, we are going to sober up and come down to the floral earth.

One (daily) wonders why they ask persons who confess to being poets to do anything else, considering the vapidity and ignorance of the breed. Except, being villainously illiterate, most painters lust for a bit of the old-fashioned cachet that word-slingers used to offer. And, *occasionally*, you do encounter a poet who will actually tell you that he doesn't know it all. In fact, that he knows it is not there to *know*. (Next week I am to struggle to say something on behalf of Frank Meadow Sutcliffe's photographs; the week after that: 3000 words on a biography of Charles Ives; the week af-

71

ter that it's a hike of the *Three Peaks Walk* and an account for *The New Yorker*, hoping to pay for the mindlessness of the three previous weeks.)

Ian Gardner is someone whose work I *respond* to. I sought it (and then him) out. I love it, and every day feels that much better because I do. So, from me you're not getting *Chachma*, as my Jewish friends say. *Wisdom* is just not turned on. I'm not about to compare Gardner to Morandi, or trace him endlessly from Cotman and Girtin, or talk about the "cognitive process" or "oneiric space." As my Jewish friends also say: "*The highest form of Wisdom is Kindness*." That I can try for.

Anyway, we are talking about an artist who sinks a few pints of Theakston's *Old Peculier* strong Yorkshire ale and then quotes you prompt pieces of Gospel. One is his own disarming remark: "*I just like pretty things!*" The other is from another Bradford lad, Gaffer David Hockney: "*Anything simple always interests me*." Yes, yes, but there is also that quotation I cannot forget from Professor Einstein: "*Everything should be as simple as it is—but not simpler*."

Well, the thing is that Our Ian is not just a wee bloke from (originally) Lancaster who has made a wee place for himself in the Art Mart. I looked through a student portfolio of his and was surprised to see that he worked through such influences as De Kooning, Kline, Albers, and the gents of the *New York City Dart Board & Awning Manufacturers Association*.

One day, sitting under a bodhi tree, or a yew or a rowan, he made a basic discovery—essentially the one that Ezra Pound made back in the days of *Imagisme* (circa 1913), to do with abstraction: *what is empty is empty, and who wants it?* EP spoke of: "Direct treatment of the 'thing,' whether subjective or objective." "Don't use an expression such as 'dim lands of *peace*.' It mixes an abstraction with the concrete. It comes from the writer's not realizing that the natural object is always the *adequate* symbol."

So, when I look at these images by Ian Gardner, there is more to it than to recall John Sell Cotman and how to lay down washes in Paynes grey and speak of the *peculiarly English* nature of it all. Or, to go on a bit, to refer back to the minute particularities of Blake and the limited scale of his *Youthful Ancients*, Samuel Palmer and Edward Calvert. Or, the size of certain Constable sketches or Charles Keene etchings.

I insisted from that start I would not interpose a critic's tiresome body between the on-looker and the lucidities of Ian Gardner's "Shoot" or "Daffodils" or "Freesia" or "Lace Tablecloth." Those (who adhere to the Goddess Hestia or the God Priapus) will have their own eyes. But, I can relate Gardner to others who might interest the self-same viewers—others beyond either side of the Pennines.

A key influence on Gardner has been the Scots poet, Ian Hamilton Finlay. Since the English mainly ignore Finlay as someone influenced by Constructivists and Suprematists and people with bizarre names like Satie and Mozart, and accuse him of being wee, twee, and whimsical, it is not odd that his anglophobia flourishes like that of his Lanarkshire neighbour, Hugh MacDiarmid. Still, he has been a whole Academy for an alert group of poets and artists in the Decadent South, and he must take (small) comfort in the fact that many of us on both sides of the Atlantic Ocean gain pleasure from him in the way we have previously gained it from Dame Edith Sitwell, D. H. Lawrence, Basil Bunting, and Stevie Smith. (May Orpheus spare me from sitting at a table with all those present at once!). Finlay has taught a sense of graphic decorum, good diction, correct scale, and devotion to one's own beloved spaces.

It will be interesting to see Ian Gardner continue his revelations of the landscape of the Yorkshire Dales. He will, obviously, not make the mistake that James Ward makes in the enormous, bewildering painting of "Gordale Scar" in the Tate. The mistake being that the real place looks mild and modest in comparison with the art work. Gardner supplies *just enough* of everything for one's own imagination to take part.

Some will say: "It's too decorative. It's too pretty. What position does it take towards free contraceptives, enosis, the next General Election and the proper hour at which to eat chip-butties???" Bill Shankly is witty enough to realise that a man is his own politics and that a painting does not score goals. William Morris said: "Have nothing in your houses that you do not know to be useful, or believe to be beautiful." Ogata Korin and the other great masters of the *rimpa* school of the late 17th century in Japan would not say Ian Gardner was *too decorative*. But I can see how people today could complain. Take those addictive, bickering, tiresome folk you hear every evening on "The Archers." Aunt Laura was quite incensed that Ambridge didn't win the Best-Kept-Village Award, after she'd worked so hard with her tongue to prettify the place. But Martha Woodford decided it was proper that Penny Hassett won, "because it's a nice, homely, tatty sort of a place." And back to the kitchen went Martha to finish off a delicious dish of rook legs in grey-grease sauce.

However, back to those with a bit of light shining out of their eyes, who've always known Beatrix Potter was a master of her chosen domain. And Gerard Manley Hopkins in his; and Ruskin, when he drew geological forms. Listen to Gaston Bachelard, the revered phenomenologist, in *The Right To Dream*. He is talking about Gardner, not just Claude Monet or Albert Flocon:

> The world asks to be seen: before ever there were eyes to see the eye of the waters, the huge eye of still waters watched the flower bloom. And it was in this reflection—who will deny it!—that the world first became aware of its beauty. Just as, from the time when Claude Monet first looked at a water lily, the water lilies of the Ile-de-France have been more beautiful, more splendid . . .

> A botany of the imagination, stemming from an attraction for branches, wood, leaves, roots, bark, flowers and grass, has furnished us with a stock of images of astonishing regularity. We are controlled by vegetal values. We would all profit by taking a census of this private herbarium in the depths of our unconscious where the slow, gentle forces of our life find models of continuity and perseverance. The life of root and bud lies at the heart of our being. We are really ancient plants.

**74**

And, then, there is that complicated, simple lady from Pittsburgh, Gertrude Stein, capable of making a giant proper Lancashire Hotch Potch of all the pleasures and pains of writing, making this crucial observation in one of her early essays:

> I remember very well when I was a little girl and I and my brother Will found as children the love poems of their very very much older brother. This older brother had just written one and it said that he had often sat and looked at any little square of grass and it had been just a square of grass as grass is, but now he was in love and so the little square of grass was all filled with birds and bees and butterflies, the difference was that love was. The poem was funny we and he knew the poem was funny but he was right, being in love made him make poetry, and poetry made him feel the things and their names . . .

Finally, three poems of Lorine Niedecker (1903–1970), a poet so quiet that hardly anyone—in all the noise, distraction, and the withered condition of his heart—has bothered yet to read. She and Ian Gardner have a way of their own making:

**MARCH**

Bird feeder's

     snow-cap

         sliding

            off.

■

Asa Gray wrote Increase Lapham:
pay particular attention
to my pets, the grasses.

■

Along the river
    wild sunflowers

over my head
     the dead
who gave me life
     gave me this
our relative the air
     floods
our rich friend
     silt.

I have put Ian Gardner among kindred spirits. Which is hoped to be also a vision of kindness.

*(From* Drawings as Prints, *A Blue Tunnel Publication, Bradford, England, 1974)*

# A PARTICULARLY NON-ARTY RESPONSE TO THE CORACLE MAN

## 1.

The man under the coracle
is:

anfractuous;
impetuous

barely capable of writing a simple declarative sentence;
barely capable of writing a poor poem

the proud owner of a formicary, deserted by ants,
now filled with fleas, which he uses for a brain

blessed with an ear like a blotter;
and a severe magpie-eye

a man who could walk on water,
if his wit weren't so dry

a catbird in a country
without any catbirds

tirelessly himself,
aloof to being cut down to size by fireless pygmies

quite impossible, and
just barely plausible

shambolic and strangely
seraphic

a wrecker,
a cracker

a wanker,
an anchor

out to lunch
long before breakfast

to be regarded with dismay and distrust
until trusted completely

ready to
do it!

## 2.

Every poet needs a *carapace*, some hard, bony, chitinous outer-covering
to protect his touchy skin and overly-soft heart from the more cretinous
members of the Great British Public and its etiolated Government, may

the Saints preserve! Mr. Simon Cutts (aka, The Scutts) uses a *coracle* for this purpose: a small, rounded boat made of waterproof material stretched over a wicker or wooden frame. The Old Welsh word for coracle was *cwrwgl*—the sort of sound Simon makes when he is exposed to some particularly grotty pint of bad ale. The Scutts snails along ceaselessly as we feckless mortals sleep . . .

Coracle is a generation younger than my own operation, the Jargon Society (1951–1989). Accordingly, by the law of the Generation Gip, we often can't figure out why we both do what we do. But, we do what we do in the most implacable of ways. Such acts don't insist that you "like" them; merely "love" them. (Goethe, it was, who asked: "What business is it of yours if I love you?") In the worldly way of the world, I should not be very interested in what this Boulevardier de Belper, Derbyshire, does with his time. Literati are all too pre-occupied with themselves and what they make. As one is really interested only in his/her birthday, his own sex life, his own feces, etc. Other people's things are *repugnant.* But, Simon Cutts and Coracle are all about *conflagration.* I can't avoid the warmth and the passion—I don't want to. *Minimal schminimal.*

Every once in awhile Simon Cutts makes a pure and simple poem (nothing is *pure* and nothing is ever *simple*, so what?)—a work I have been waiting for all my life to see. Now and then he makes a book that seems inevitable and utterly right. Once in awhile he plops down a dozen exquisite Norfolk oysters and a bottle of 1983 Sancerre. It is, thus, a privilege to be alive at the same time as this admirable bugger; and to be in the presence of such artifice. There is little nowadays that is not venal, silly, captious, cold, or worth one's abiding affection. Coracle provides both protection and pleasure.

**SEE ORACLE! CARPE DIEM! CARPET YOUR CARAPACE!**

*(From* The Coracle, *Coracle Press Gallery, 1975–1987, an exhibition at the Yale Centre for British Art, New Haven, CT, 1989)*

# "WE ALL LIVE IN A
# YELLOW SUBMAROON"

I owe my discovery of Spike Hawkins' poems to Ian Hamilton Finlay. A few lines would stray into *Poor.Old.Tired.Horse.*, now and then, and quite bemuse me. Who is this Hawkins? I asked. Finlay said: "Aye, super wee poems, but he's very wild . . ." From Pete Brown, poet and writer of rock lyrics, I learned that S. Hawkins lived in the village of Heath and Reach, near Leighton Buzzard, Bedfordshire—not a place, somehow, one ever reckoned to visit. Very wild, indeed.

Here are are couple of super wee poems:

### BOILER

Pig sit still in the strainer!
Pig sit still in the strainer!
I must have my pig tea!

### TREE ARMY POEM

Alert Ruin!
they shout from the trees.
Stupid bloody acorns!

## SPRUNG

the ratfish trap
hangs in the hall
waiting until morning
when I feel ratty

## I SENT A RICH LETTER

Tasha I have won the goblet
and the free rosy plinth.
Melissa sent a cable from
the Caribbean, it says "Gratters".
The castle dance did swing,
Were you tiddly, I mean stoned?
Bunny Tucker is a stinker!
Come and see my Goblet,
I'm not washing since I
had the presentation
Man!

There matters stood, and/or sat, etc., until a pride of poets collected in Nottingham in February, 1966, under the auspices of Stuart Mills and Martin Parnell, proprietors of the Trent Bookshop. I found myself the compère at a Friday night poetry & jazz session, which included a sloshed Spike Hawkins.

The Hawkins vocal attack is unique: a mixture of Aubrey Beardsley (whom he resembles) and Mick Jagger. But more delicate than that, snarling the punch line with one long leg flicking out, as Peter Osgood might slip a pass to Tambling, heading full-tilt towards the Liverpool goal. These poems must be snarled, yelled, danced, and enforced—they are neither demure, nor "balanced," nor predictable. Neither are they the "deliberate goonery" of which they have been accused. Like the poems of Stevie Smith (among the maternal ancestors), their surface is light, witty, ever mindful of the fact that words are being put together. Underneath, Stevie Smith is invariably touching upon an instance of pain. Spike Hawkins, invariably, is asking questions of "sanity"—now you have it, now you don't.

A Hawkins poem is a talisman against the rubbish of the Average Mind, the One that infests the world in horrifically increasing numbers. Last night I sat at table in the *S. S. Rotterdam*'s dining room and heard one crusty, jew-baiting, nigger-hating female, out of North Dakota, by way of Juno, Alaska, spew precisely this concatenation of sentences, I kid you not: "Of course, the problem in Alaska is that the indians and the eskimos don't pay any fucking taxes. Well, anyway, when we moved to Arlington, Virginia, we decided to have our daughter, Susie (the one with the red Porsche, not the one who played five times with the National Symphony when she was 16 and even the orchestra applauded her), have her portrait painted by Henk Bluttwurst, the famous Dutch artist (he called her "The Queen")—you know, don't you, young man, that he once painted Jackie Kennedy in the famous Rubenstein Style, so lovely, well, it's a very large, genuine oil portrait . . . Say, do you think that darky over there (I'd say he's some kind of african) is married to that white girl? They certainly seem to be seeing a lot of each other. Imagine—on a ship like the *Rotterdam*!"

That is an Average Mind at work, and upon such rock-heads is the Modern World divinely founded. Give me a "nut" like old Spike Hawkins any day—a few more of them, and the planet might go on. A couple more recent poems by The Spike:

### RICK

There is a bed in
Thursford Green
Whose heat is mine
Whose Hay I watered

## STREETWISE

I met Love on the Town road.
It writes as you said it would.
Where I would have stopped in the suburbs
it went on, writing.

## CAMBRIDGE TOWELS

The gnats wore iron
that evening
on the nearby river
lit with splinters.
We clapped under the
bridge for the acts
that never arrived
and later retired
to Esher for a well
deserved path bark.

These words were once designed to be the brief introduction to a Jargon book we would call *Spike Hawkins Versus the Bat People & Other Bloody Poems.* A wee volume to follow upon *Spike Hawkins Poems* (Tarasque Press, Nottingham, 1966) and *The Lost Fire Brigade* (Fulcrum Press, London, 1968). Somehow it never happened. If video took away literature and its audience, it was because we were too careless, too meagre, too reluctant to get bloody thumb out, mate.

I could (*and still can*) read Spike Hawkins. The poems contain fresh lines. Strangely, they help hold what I call "my world" together. Mr. Hawkins still hangs on, in a suburb of London known as Finchley. I don't see him; nobody sees him. I can get no poet to go knock on his door and ask for the poems since 1968. The fragility of the whole thing is more than enough to bring tears to the eyes. Pete Brown, Spike's friend and talented contemporary, once said something sharp and of interest to all of us inept persons:

they should really have farms
for poets poets should be like cows
milked twice a day
& those that don't produce should be eaten

*(Unpublished, 1969–1991)*

# BILL ANTHONY'S GREATEST HITS, BY WILLIAM ANTHONY

When I read a title of a drawing like "The Artist Teaching Laurent Weichberger, Age Nine, How To Dance Like Frankenstein," I know we're someplace *special* in the company of a very special high-wired aerialist and anti-artiste. No doubt about it, Bill Anthony, like the one-legged man at an ass-kicking contest, is in a league by himself. Can you dig it?

To indicate there are still a few hold-outs who do not believe that Bill Anthony is the Cosmo-Demonic Lead-Pencil Leonardo da Shaky *de nos jours*, I quote a letter from that most estimable of philosophers, W. H. Ferry: "I *cannot*, dear Jonathan, join the admirers of Bill Anthony. I'm too old, or too young, or too arty, or too holy, or too something. I cannot, moreover, understand why *anyone*... etc." John Russell was so appalled by Anthony's *Bible Stories* that he dared not speak to me for two years.

And yet, and yet... the distinguished art critic & historian, Robert Rosenblum, is the man introducing this bumper crop of *Bill Anthony's Greatest Hits*. As he says, "It's an odd angle of vision that levels all our activities, whether high art or low life, to a plane of behavior so inconsequentially silly that we can only laugh, not cry, at our follies, even when they include the Second World War." Other illuminated fans include R. B. Kitaj, Roy Lichtenstein, and the late Thomas B. Hess. These are *tough* hombres, O gentle readers, and recognize a full-bore bull-goose pseudo-loony when they see one.

It is late at night. In a lonely house on the edge of the Land of Yup, I hear a hideous scraping noise as Bill Anthony's pencil climbs the stair—O Nightmare Vision! O Crawling Horror! Good Golly, Miss Molly!

We hope there are a few thousand of you who will cease your tireless efforts carving portrait busts of recent American presidents out of petrified bat guano, who will look at this book and see what a weird & wonderful talent is here on dreadful display.

*(Blurb for Jargon 90, 1988)*

# CLERIHEWS

The *clerihew* was invented in 1890 by Edmund Clerihew Bentley, who was a schoolboy of 16 at St. Paul's in London when the divine numen of Orpheus struck him. His best one seems to me:

> The digestion of Milton
> Was unequal to Stilton.
>
> He was only feeling so-so
> When he wrote Il Penseroso.

He never got any better than that, and few people have ever managed to equal him, though such as Auden, John Sparrow, Constant Lambert, James Elroy Flecker, Maurice Hare and Gavin Ewart have tried. I can recall one sublime effort:

> How odd
> of God
>
> to choose
> the Jews.

But I can never remember the English war poet who wrote it. This makes me quote the equally sublime contradiction by Leo Rosten:

Not odd
of Gód.

Goyim
annoy'im!

E. C. Bentley went on to Oxford, was a life-long friend of G .K. Chesterton, wrote editorials for *The Daily Telegraph* for more than twenty years, and is remembered as the author of the detective novel, *Trent's Last Case.*

Francies Stillman's *The Poet's Manual and Rhyming Dictionary* (1966) says this: "The clerihew is a humorous pseudo-biographical quatrain, rhymed as two couplets, with lines of uneven length, and often contains or implies a moral reflection of some kind. The name of the individual who is the subject of the quatrain usually supplies the first line."

# THE CLERIHEWS
# OF CLARA HUGHES

Never read James Dickey
when the weather's hot and icky.

The time for dickey-dunkin
's when de frost is on de punkin.

Babe Ruth
in all truth

weren't borned like you an' me—
he come down out of a tree.

Hesiod
is seldom read.

His *Works & Days*
irks most guys.

Stevie Smith
invited Death

to live with her
and eat verdure.

Mombi the Witch
had an itch

to be a Girl Goddess
like Robert Duncan in his eleusinian, pearl headdress.


Ezra Loomis Pound
bought a lb

of Idaho potatoes
(the Hailey Comet always ate those).


Why did Professor J. R. R. Tolkien
never really come clean

about the scientologists in cupboards
in the House of L. Ron Hubbard?


Li Tai Po,
please telepho-

ne Mnemosyne,
straight away!


David Hockney
met a most ravissant Cockney

with, *mirabile dictu,*
no cock to hang onto!


Hank D. Thoreau
too seldom used eau

de Cologne,
and was asked to live at Walden on his own.

Sir Edward Elgar
was never vulgar,

though why—in mixed company—he made jokes about smegma
was certainly an enigma.

Percy Grainger
was no stranger

to stinging whips
and Mother's lips.

Puccini
is arguably better than zucchini.

But a pound of spinach
could write a better symphony than Zdenek Fibich.

Ross Lee Finney
left North Dakota because he wasn't getting any

Tartini, dodecaphony
or even weeny.

They say Herman "The Hunk" Melville was given to itches
to get into Mr. Nathaniel Hawthorne's britches.

But, there is no evidence that Queequeg
ever went whole hog.

John Blow
was below

par when he wrote *Cloe Found Amintas Lying
On a Pile of Swedes Near Dorking.*

## APPLE-PIE ORDER

Mr. Charles Edward Ives
vies

with Spike Jones, John Philip Sousa, and Scott Joplin
for being the number one All-American.

Ralph Vaughan Williams
munches now on trilliums . . .

Having contrived in earthly clay just how
to write sweet music very like a cow.

John Cage
bestrode his age.

"FUCK ZEN!"
chimes in the octogenarian Huck Finn.

Charles Tomlinson Griffes
was said to have the stiffest

dork
in refined musical circles in all of Elmira, New York.

Alma Mahler
could really holler!

On those odd, ur-Freudian occasions when she took it up the butt,
she often hit fortissimo high-C and commenced doing the "Danube
    Strut."

Leos Janacek
in photographs looks a bloody blank Czech.

His music, as it unfurls,
appeals mostly to squirrels.

Franz Liszt
even played the piano when he pissed.

It was odd to see his piano stool dripping
during performances of *Années de Pèlerinage* that were
  absolutely gripping!

### "THE BARON"

Both bodacious & humongous
was large Charles Mingus.

On both mouth & bass-
he played his ass.

Thomas Wolfe
wolfed

herds
of words

Said Morgan Foster
over some oysters:

"Only Connect-
icut!"

### NEAR WHINNY HAW

Climbing Firbank Fell,
Ronald Firbank fell

about laughing
at two heifers fucking.

### SUNT LACHRYMAE RERUM

The truth is William Blake
is hard to take

for those of us with earthy ears
and eyes the size of tiny deer's.

### LES MATINS DANS LA RUE DE FLEURUS, NO.27

Gertrude Stein
arose at nine

and arose and arose
and arose

Clara Hughes, the author of these clerihews,
wrote them strictly to chase the Blues.

"Gee, I think they're neat,"
said her illiterate girl friend, Pete.

*(Many of these clerihews were published as*
The Fifty-Two Clerihews of Clara Hughes,
*Pynyon Press, Atlanta, 1983. Thanks to Tom*
*Patterson, Publisher, for permission to reprint.)*

94

# CLARENCE JOHN LAUGHLIN

*A Memorial Piece, in the Formal Manner of*

*Louis Moreau Gottschalk's "The Dying Poet," Styled with*

*the Hubris of Ferdinand "Jelly Roll" Morton and the Insolence*

*of W. C. Fields, entitled Clarence in Wonderland—no,*

*make that Clarence in Wonder (bread) land; or, "Fondled by*

*Fate's Fickle Finger, Crushed by the Quirks of Time . . ."*

Those old enough to remember Zazu Pitts, Alf Landon, chain-gangs, Necco wafers, and Dr. Zharkov, from the Planet Mongo, will also remember the character-actor, Thomas Mitchell, in numerous jungle epics of the silver screen where he played the rummy, grizzled, Irish doctor, captured by Hottentots, Ubangis, Watusi, et al., and gone totally to seed. To the sudden sound of drums and spear-rattling, explorers arrive in the village clearing, and he whispers to anyone stupid enough to listen: "I'm the only white man the natives trust." Seldom does the language rise to such farcical heights. Jack Gelber used the line to superb account in *The Connection*, which I saw in the first Living Theater production back in the late 1950s. That's about when I met Clarence John Laughlin (younger than I am now), and it still sums him up precisely and flawlessly.

Cousin Clarence was, as we say in Southern parlance, a real catbird, a sight-and-a-half. I am finding it hard to imagine this piece of raw real-estate we call America with him not there in the catbird seat, because, for me and a surprising number of others, Clarence John Laughlin did more than anyone else to record and salvage and cherish a civilization on this continent that has been almost destroyed in just two generations. He worked harder, against more stupid obstacles, than any artist I've ever met—over fifty years on the job. Never enough space, never enough time, never enough money, never enough (worst of all) serious response. The Ford Foundation and the MacArthur Foundation were never clever enough to ferret him out. The New York Establishment never gave this inspired bumpkin a major exhibition. (To be fair to the excellent eye of Julien Levy, prints by CJL were in a group show at his East 57th Street gallery in 1940.) The federal bureaucracy should have made him a "National Treasure" decades ago.

Who could he talk to in New Orleans? The Kingfish, Big Jim Garrison, Bum Philips? Unfortunately, interesting local men like Roark Bradford and Bill Russell trafficked only with black stories and black music. Clarence came out of a time and place that generally agreed with Harold Ross, Editor of *The New Yorker* in those days: "Coons are either funny or dangerous." And so it is doubtful he ever met, or knew, the great instrumentalists who were his contemporaries in the Crescent City: George Lewis, Jim Robinson, "Slow Drag" Pavageau, Baby Dodds, Lawrence Marrero, Kid Thomas, Emile Barnes, "One-Eyed-Babe" Philips, Billie & DeDe Pierce, and so many others.

Clarence John Laughlin, Baudelaire of the Bayous, had all the credentials to become a triumphant American weird. "Just an eye, but what an eye," someone said about Monet. It is with the French that one links him, and there was French blood in his veins when he was born in Lake Charles, Louisiana, in 1905. He revered Atget. He became as much an eidolon as Odilon Redon. He was "spooked" by the adult world of hard-nosed businessmen. He was "tetched in the haid," as we say down South. One of God's fools, the perpetual, pre-rational enthusiast, who saw there was more than met any *normal* eye. Eye that meat, Cousin Clarence! "I'm the only Extreme Romantic Imagination the natives trust . . ."

When Bette Midler once played "The Frog and Nightgown" in Raleigh, North Carolina, she found Fuquay-Varina and asked: "What's hot in Fuquay-Varina?" Some wit took her to the automatic carwash on Saturday morning, where the studs make them suds. Cousin Clarence—in

Fuquay-Varina the same day—never having heard of the Divine Miss Midler, would have ignored the bouncing mammaries and, instead, would have combed the flea markets, finding rare first editions of Abe Merritt's *The Moon Pool* and *Dwellers in the Mirage*, and *Seven Footprints to Satan*, where tits-and-ass prose parades cosmic hoochi-coochi from the planets of the Dark Galaxy, etc., etc. "I'm the only white man who remembers who wrote *The Moon Pool.*"

One imagines that it would not have taken Clarence John long in Fuquay-Varina to find out about Clyde "Jungle Boy" Jones's outdoor sculpture garden in Bynum, on the Haw River, what Clyde calls his "Haw River Critter Crossing"; or to get wind of the outlandish structure known as "Butt's Dream House" in a clump of tattered trees near Moyock, some miles northeast of Elizabeth City, North Carolina. En route, he would have stopped in Rocky Mount, not because Jim Thorpe played minor-league ball there or because Thelonious Sphere Monk was born there, but because of an elusive gentleman named Vernon Burwell, retired from railway work, whose sculptures (conglutinations of cement over coat-hangers and painted with enamels from the hardware store) will scare you to death. "Man Eating Banana" looks more like "Tyrannosaurus Eating a Man." Real Clarence meat.

Hold on. That's not fair to Clarence. He would have had some Thelonious Sphere Monk, if only because the sublime name shook his antennae. The reason Clarence didn't like music was because he never shut up and listened to any. This did not prevent him from collecting hundreds of (unplayed) albums by composers he claimed for his own by intuition: Abel Decaux, Alkan, Berwald, Delius, Gottschalk, Koechlin, Dane Rudhyar . . .

Laughlin would argue that the trouble with Edward Weston was that he only saw "what was there." Harry Callahan would argue that the trouble with Clarence John Laughlin was that he only saw "what wasn't there." Photographers are full of it, like poets, and would do better to focus their righteousness, mendation, and mentation on money-markets,

Madonna's cleavage, and the earned-run average of the pitching staff of the Atlanta Braves: "Now you see it, now you don't." Wonderful, and wonderfully typical, of Clarence to declare himself the "Photographer of the Third World," never having twigged that all those a-rabs, orientals, and blackamoor chappies are referred to as the Third World by the entire Western World except CJL. Laughlin, like Carnaki the Ghost-Finder in William Hope Hodgson's stories, was a very singular sleuth.

Laughlin explored the territory of "The Strange" like some people might go to something called "The Country" for the weekend. But his St. Louis, or Milwaukee, or Memphis, would be no one else's. He ate his poorboy sandwiches, drank his Dr. Pepper, and thought about Redon, not about *Galatoire's* or *LeRuth's*. He read all the wackier "poetic" stuff of his period. People, myself included, used to get off on such batty drivel as these lines from Henry Miller: "We taxi from one perfect female to the next, seeking their vulnerable defects, but they are flawless and impermeable in their impeccable lunar consistency . . ." And whatever New Orleans was in Clarence Laughlin's dreams, in fact it was a sultry, somewhat dangerous, crass river town, full of liberated conventioneers, and the usual bourgeois insensitivities; i.e., Almost Everywhere Else '85. What else was ever new?

Clarence John Laughlin animates the world more for those of us the natives don't trust on this stormy October day than he ever did during his nearly eighty years. He still gives us pause to wonder. Last week I looked off a barge on the Canal du Midi in Languedoc and saw, outlined in the bark of a plane tree at Capestang, the fantastic profile and features of Dante. There it is, captured on the spot by SX-70 film, in the manner of Archimboldo. CLJ came to mind a few minutes later reading a crime novel by the excellent English writer Ruth Rendell: "Linthea, a Jamaican, a beauty, a social worker, who had no ties, who lived in and worked for a society she understood, who wasn't effete with poetry and dream and metaphor and a jelly-like sensitivity that melts at a hard touch." The Hard World allows very few Clarences to probe its dreams.

I salute him for the washtub of glorious, eldritch, preternatural, gumbo he was. "There's an eye in the sky watchin' you!" Clarence, how much I wish I could take you to Pennville, Georgia, and let the Rev. Howard Finster pick you that tune on his banjo and then walk you through his New-Improved Garden of Eden. But it's too late. The Laughlins and Eugène Atgets of this world are noble and go invisibly. I can just hear Clarence on the streetcar to Elysian Fields telling Atget what he's been missing, and how: "We're the only coon-asses the immortals trust!"

*(Aperture 103, New York, 1986)*

# WILD GOULD CHASE

My taste for the literary strays and mavericks has been engorged over the years by ceaseless ramblings about the USA and Great Britain by car and on foot. H. P. Lovecraft was the first weird I clutched to my bosom (age 14) and I can't get his preternatural presence out of my system even now 30 years later. As the public taste for Mahler and Bruckner and Nielsen and Satie and Ives and Elgar and Delius blossoms in the manner of the Night-Blooming Cereus and the Century Plant, I feel relieved of evangelical duties and begin to wander down curious, weedy paths marked C. T. Griffes, Cyril Scott, Lord Berners, Sorabji, Iggy Pop, Scott Joplin, and (early) Earl Scruggs. Perhaps more important than this exclusivity, randomness, and/or quirkiness is a recognition how *fragile* such an art as poetry is in the vacuous, disinterested, commercial deluge of today. This was brought home recently when it took almost a month for me to learn of the death of Lorine Niedecker, at 67, in Fort Atkinson, Wisconsin—this, despite the fact I publish the lady and that there are more than a few poets who feel she was the best of her sex since Emily Dickinson. It seems that only Basil Bunting, Louis Zukofsky, and Guy Davenport had received this sad news in all America. There was no obituary in the *New York Times* and no public notice at all, except in the local paper in Wisconsin. But, what can one do? As someone says, it's like yelling at fungus. Better to walk around it and move on.

Robert Kelly has remarked how depressingly like the destruction of native American architecture is the deliberate, callous, trendy, beady-eyed view of The Reading Public, ah gentle fiction, toward poets and their unread works. Edward Arlington Robinson must give way to William Carlos Williams; Dr. Williams must give way to Robert Creeley; Creeley must give way to whom?—Leonard Cohen, Rod McKuen, Richard Brautigan???? One doesn't like to think. Russell Edson, a lonely writer of lonely fables for 20 years, said the other day: "My brand of writing (the short prose poem) is being *re-discovered*, and even poets, gosh Poets, are not unmindful of my silly inventions. Of course this is all no more than the length of women's skirts. We Americans are like a shallow dish of water—the slightest tilt . . ."

The Jargon Society has been this one goliardic poet's immodest effort to combat inattention, both from academic jocks and the plastic urbane. Hugh Kenner muttered darkly one night in Spiro T. Agnew's hometown that I was "The Custodian of Snowflakes" and implied that I had about as much chance as a snowball in hell of "establishing" such deliquescent poets. It certainly can be so argued. Where once I was concerned with getting out some of the early books of Charles Olson, Robert Creeley, Robert Duncan, Denise Levertov, Louis Zukofsky, Irving Layton, Buckminster Fuller, the current arcanum includes Niedecker and Edson (mentioned previously), Thomas Meyer, Ross Feld, Alfred Starr Hamilton, Richard Emil Braun, Ronald Johnson, Mason Jordan Mason, James Broughton, Paul Metcalf, Douglas Woolf, Guy Davenport and across the Atlantic: Ian Gardner, John Furnival, and Tom Phillips. (We will now have an interlude of exotic music by Cyril Scott as the Reading Public lines up with dollars for this lot.)

Reading William Carlos Williams' *Autobiography,* one day back in the late 50s, I caught the good doctor carrying on about the poems of a huge character from Maine named Wallace Gould. Marsden Hartley had introduced the two of them. WCW wrote: "I was fascinated by the poems' romantic tenor, I suppose, but there was more than that to them. Gould used the local material in a broad way with loose, undulant lines that I greatly admired. In fact, it was not the nostalgic glamour of these Victorian passages at all, but the firmness of their images and a smoothness of diction that I praised to Margaret Anderson and Jane Heap." That's about all that Dr. Williams said, except to tell some anecdotes about this 300-pound, one-quarter Abnaki Indian, who ended his days in Farmville, Virginia, baking three kinds of pound cake and playing piano at the local silent movie house in order to live.

With bait from the likes of WCW and Marsden Hartley, I thought I might have me a genuine snowflake on the line. After all, it was simply running into a sentence in a letter from Pound to Marianne Moore, written in 1921, that set me off earlier in pursuit of Mina Loy's vanished poems: "Also, entre nooz: is there anyone in America except you, Bill and Mina Loy who can write anything of interest in verse?" That clue, plus a little essay by Kenneth Rexroth in *Circle* back in the 40s.

Scholars were of no help at all—dozing in their carrels, trying to decide whether it was finally safe to devote some time and money to the septuagenarian Dr. Williams, or maybe better stick to the poets sacred to *Time* magazine. Yep, it was the *poets*, the "Company of Friends," as ever, who were keeping the lines of communication (alias the made poem) trickling bleakly from one generation to the next. During the 15 years since Jargon Society brought out 500 copies of Mina Loy's *Lunar Baedeker & Timetables,* only two nibbles from the Academy. A gent surfaced at Stanford, went to LA, and vanished. However, at the University of Iowa a student of Sherman Paul's, Virginia Kouidis, has stuck to it, done important spade work, unearthed lost poems, and written a dissertation. She deserves our thanks.

Back to W. Gould. I began to wonder what to do, how to find his work and gauge his quality. A lucky thing happened. I had a letter from Bill Harmon, a poet from down in Concord, North Carolina. He was then (summer of 1960) on leave from the Navy. I knew him only by letter but knew he was a keen disciple of the Pound/Wms ways & means. So I said: Doc Wms is himself keen on thishere Gould. Get yourself up the road to Farmville and see what the news is. He said: Why not? My grandparents live in a place called Motley, Virginia, not too far away. I'll do the two-bird one-stone thing . . .

So here is what we found out for ourselves (alias Posterity) about Wallace Chester Gould:

*Dear Jargon,*
I thought I'd wait to make up my WG document until I'd had a look at WCW's account (or whatever) of Gould so I'd know what you know and don't know and so wouldn't be wasting this fine yellow 5 for a cent paper on tales that would turn out to be twice-told. But what the hell, I'll outline (1) my procedure and (2) my findings—all for naught anyhow because more than likely poor dead Gould isn't worth much anyway.

Bus from Altavista to Lynchburg, arriving there about 9:30 (this is Thursday, about July 7th) and finding that I had to change from Trailways to Greyhound and the latter bus didn't leave until 1:20; so I went to the Jones Memorial Library across this big bridge in Lynchburg, and whatdoyouknow! they had a copy of Gould's *Aphrodite*, to wit:

Wallace Gould: *Aphrodite and Other Poems*, NY, The Macaulay Company, MCMXXVII.

Flyleaf inscribed in black ink, handwriting nearly illegible (from boldness, not from trembliness):

Corrected and revised by The Author July 1, 1929.

The book dedicated to Alfred Kreymborg, with a foreword consisting of three worse than soso sonnets by AK.

I also (still in the Jones Mem. Lib.) looked at a copy of *An Anthology of American Poetry: Lyric America: 1630–1941*, edited by Alfred Kreymborg (Tudor Pub. Co., NY, 1941, 2nd Rev. Edition) which has (on pp. 463–471) five poems (all from *Aphrodite*) by Wallace G . . .

And the Librarian (who'd never heard of WG but wanted to help, esp. so when I told her I was Robert Frost) found for me this:

*The New Republic:* Wed Dec 26, 1928 (Vol. LVII No. 734), where (on pp. 171–2) appeared a review "Three Poets" by Melvin P. Levy, who praised WG highly but called A. Kreymborg's three introductory sonnets "execrable."

Had a good lunch then in the Virginian Restaurant, a beer at the Virginia Grill, and so to Farmville. Sort of rat's-ass little town, pop. 4300, home of Longwood College, mostly for girls but with a few male day students. Went first to that college's esteemed and (in more than architecture) Georgian library, where nobody had heard of Gould—but their copy of *Aph* was checked out; so then to the little public library (in the cool cellar of an old house, with an old librarian) and was told yes yes yes of course Wallace Gould, oh my goodness, but I can't tell you much about him; why don't you try Horace Adams, County Clerk, and Barry Wall, ed.-pub. of *Farmville Herald?*

Mr. Wall was not in his office at the *Herald* so I went to the courthouse (i.e., COVRTHOVSE) and Mr. Horace Adams couldn't say much, so sent me next door to the municipal building.

There I met Mr. William Gills, city treasurer, who took me in his Plymouth (?1956) out to the cemetery (called, I think, Westview) to plot 95 where I viewed the simple grave of the aforementioned Mr. Gould, and also his wife's.

Back then to Mr. Gills's office where he called up his 80yr old mother to see if she knew anything about WG, having been one of his (i. e., WG's) wife's best friends; she told him that I should see Dr. Whitaker, Gould's closest friend in Fville, but nobody answered the phone at the Dr.'s so Mr. Gills then called the *Herald* office, where Mr. Wall was by then, and told him I was coming over.

At the *Herald* office I met Mr. Wall, talked awhile with him, copied out the obit notice they had run on WG, and then he mentioned Dr. Whitaker again and said he was eccentric and maybe just wouldn't answer the phone, so just took me out there in his Ford (?1803) car.

Dr. Lloyd D. Whitaker was discovered in the backyard garden of his home tending cucumbers and grapes. Mr. Wall left me with him, having business in town. Dr. Whitaker also writes poems (bad newspaper stuff; he knows it) and constructs evilly hard mechanical puzzles (see article on puzzles in *Scientific American* about Sept 59—mentions Dr. Whitaker) in his retirement (he's between 70 and 80, a self-proclaimed "non-conformist," proving it by pointing out three framed quotations on his study wall, 2 Emersons and 1 Elbert Hubbard) . . . he and I talked about Gould for about an hour, and then I called up Mr. Wall and he sent his son out in his Henry J (?1955) car to get me, and soon (I had arrived in Fville a little after 3 pm) I caught the 7:40 bus to Lynchburg (then a Trailways to Altavista, but it wasn't a local so wasn't going to stop in Motley where my grandparents live so shitshitshitshitshit I had to walk the 4 or 5 miles to Motley, not far but up 2 long steep hills, and it was raining a little, trying to hitchhike but nobody stopping, arriving home at midnight, folded, spindled, and mutilated, feet ablister, headache, pockets afull of scrawly notes etc.)

But, now the stuff on WG himself, which I garnered all over, having been told among other things by Dr. Whitaker, who knew Gould better than anybody, that I knew all there was to know because he hadn't talked much about himself; so the story is pretty dim . . . still, WG's life seems much more interesting than his poetry; although his poetry could be worse. I guess . . .

b. 1882 in Lewiston, Maine, presumably of a good family, attended pub. schools & McGill University. Planned to study for the Catholic priesthood but developed into an atheist. Then messed around with the idea of being a concert pianist. Dim days: alcohol, narcotics, women, and finally in about 1919 came (for reasons unknown—Dr. Whitaker thinks from some of G's poems that it was an unhappy love affair) to Virginia and lived in Cumberland, a tiny place just across the Appomattox Riv. from Farmville. Walked into Farmville one day wearing the first knickers ever seen in those parts & got a job playing piano in the Eaco Movie House (Eaco, pronounced Echo, standing for Educational Amusement Corp.) holding that job until about 1928 or 29. In 1932, at the age of 50, he married Miss Mary Jackson (then 52 years old) and they lived together until one day he died suddenly while chopping wood.

He was very talented and intelligent but purposeless, and he would take up one pursuit enthusiastically and abandon it soon after. Apparently his

**105**

wife had money. For one spell, before his marriage, Gould kept a great many cats (estimates range from 10 to 30; see poems in *Aph*, esp. what is probably the best thing in the book, "The Penitents") but one day killed all of them. Mr. Wall's son suggested to me that a paper had been written on Gould by a girl at Longwood College, mentioning that there were "homosexual tendencies." Not much more to say. Died Dec. 3, 1940. His life paralleled Joyce's chronologically, almost to the month:

GOULD    b. Mar 18, 1882    d. Dec 3, 1940

JOYCE    b. Feb 2, 1882    d. Jan 13, 1941

As Kreymborg's sonnets suggest, he was over 6 feet tall and weighed a lot more than 200 pounds. Dr. Whitaker (who, since he owned the Eaco Theater, was G's employer as well as his friend) says he did not look like the sort of person he was.

From the *Farmville Herald*, Dec. 6, p. 3:

### W. C. GOULD DIED TUESDAY AFTERNOON

Wallace Chester Gould, 58, author, poet and musician, died suddenly about 5 o'clock Tuesday afternoon at his home in Cumberland County across the Appomattox River from Farmville. Funeral services were held Thursday afternoon at 2 o'clock from the Doyne Funeral Home. Rev. A. H. Hollingsworth, Jr., pastor of the Presbyterian Church, officiated. Interment was in the Farmville cemetery.

Mr. Gould is survived by his widow, who was, before her marriage to him in 1932, Miss Mary Jackson, of Farmville.

Mr. Gould was born March 18, 1882, in Lewistown, Maine. He was educated in the public schools of Lewiston and at McGill University in Canada. He showed artistic ability as a poet and as a musician and had several books of poems published. His writings were of a high order and critics voted him among the best.

Mr. Gould came to Virginia about twenty years ago and had lived in Cumberland County ever since . . .

I am reminded to remark that Farmville is in Prince Edward County, and the folks kind of liked to think of G as a Yankee intruder from across the river. Dr. Whitaker said that Mr. Gould (everybody called him Mr. Gould to me, and never Wallace or, god forbid, Wally, but from respect or habit or cus-

**106**

tom or what I don't know) was very profane and would readily in any company rail against religion which he said was "god damned bullshit."

Gould's tombstone and his wife's are the same shape and size. Plot 95. As you face west, his is on the left and hers on the right; their feet towards the east. The stones are small, maybe 18" by 12", four spots of birdshit chiaroscuro on his; the stones are about 8 inches apart, and between them sits an empty rusty jar that once I suppose held flowers, but now just weedy . . .

and that's my large adventure:
Woollylamb Halfmoon in
Gouldsville, U.S.A.
with 11 fullpage halftones
by "Phiz"
introduction by
Morton Dauwen Zabel
& when I see WCW's *Autobiog* I'll see what I missed or omitted or forgot.

William Harmon (his mark)

*July 12, 1960*
*Pinkerton's Agency*
Corncob, N. Carolina

*Allen, Baby,*
You done real good in goul Virginny. Of course, we *still* don't know why WCW spends so much time on Mr. G . . . I located one more title, *Children of the Sun: Rhapsodies & Poems,* The Cornhill Company, Boston, 1917, dedicated to Marsden Hartley. Well, it's a hell of a lot better than *Aphrodite* but, gee, that's not hard. There *must* be other stuff, somewhere . . . I ran across a reference to Gould in Kenneth Rexroth's NYTBR piece on Eli Siegel and Louis Zukofsky: "perhaps Williams was so enthusiastic because the poems (it's Siegel's poems he means) resemble the work of a very good poet only he and I seem to remember—Wallace Gould. That is, they are a sort of whimsical, wistfully clownish reworking of certain of the more outstanding of the devices of the Whitman idiom—a Whitman who is no longer able to take his bright-eyed gospel very seriously, but who still thinks it is about the best . . ."

**107**

So, please keep me on. *Jargon* will roll the stone back from the tomb if there's anybody in there.

J.W.

July 16, 1960

*Dear General Grant,*

Gouldiana continues . . . I wrote to Dr. Whitaker (veterinarian/Farmville) about WCW's *Autobiography* on the chance that he hadn't read it, including big quotations; and asked him to comment on them. And he said:

> Received your 7/15 letter and I thank you for sending me quotations from *The Autobiography of William Carlos Williams.* While I have not read this book, I recall that Gould talked to me about it and let me glance through it.

(Now since Gould died in 1940 and W's *Autobiog* came out about 1951, what could Gould have talked to Dr. Whitaker about?)

More:

> Some of the things told about Gould in this book may or may not be true. For instance, it tells about him while in New York, either trembling with fright or not far from it. And also about him being too frightened to draw his hand away from a woman's breast who was evidently trying to seduce him. This is not in keeping with the way I sized him up. I can't imagine him acting the Joseph part. From what I knew of him, I can't imagine him being scared of a woman. In fact he told me about himself and another fellow taking a girl to the woods and robbing her of her maidenhead not by force but with her cooperation and consent . . .

> The Miss Mary Jackson referred to was a former school teacher who was a member of one of our oldest and best known families. She was an intelligent woman and upon meeting Gould fell violently in love with him. From me, she bought a small farm with a two-room shack on it and gave it to Gould long before she induced him to marry her. She spent all she possessed on Gould to make her his wife and that she

died a virgin, I have no doubt in my mind that this is true. I know for a fact that the only reason Gould married her was to get a meal ticket. For the last few years of his life, he did nothing and Miss Mary took care of him, lavishing upon him every penny she owned.

So?

Agent Harmon, out

*July 21, 1960*


So, indeed, 1973, there pretty much it stands. If some back-water scholar can enlighten us with a horde of good Gould poems, he'd better come forward. Us poets may have flubbed it. The last thing I did was to drive to Farmville from a reading in Charlottesville. Must have been in September, 1962. I found the old town cemetery, parked along the highway, and grabbed my Rolleiflex. Not having agent Harmon's brief in hand, I stumbled about for half an hour in the weeds and found no sign of the grave. Back across the road opposite the entrance to Westview was a cluster of shacks occupied by, in local parlance, field niggers. I figured, maybe somebody over there took care of the cemetery now and then and could help me. So I walked over and approached some men sitting on the front porch. It was Sunday afternoon, "Excuse me," I said, "does anyone happen to know about a man named Wallace Gould buried across the road and where the grave might be?" A couple of older gents shuffled their feet, a couple flicked cigar ashes, and nobody said a word. Now why the hell was that? And then it came to me: Farmville, PRINCE EDWARD COUNTY, Virginia, the *one* place in the United States of America that had closed all public schools for both races in 1959 in order to dodge integration. So much for the social effect after three such years: nobody felt like saying yassuh or nossuh to no white boy in a black dude cap and New York plates on his orange VW. I went back to the cemetery and finally found what I wanted. R.I.P., W.C.G.

One other time in my life have I been fed a ration of public silence.

Since the episode dovetails in precisely with matters of poetry and prejudice, I tell it.

The occasion was the 71st birthday of Ezra Pound. Jargon had just published Louis Zukofsky's *Some Time*. Robert Creeley and I were returning by car from New York to Black Mountain College. Zukofsky wrote a card ahead to Pound, saying that we hoped to speak with him and that I was carrying an inscribed copy of LZ's book for EP . . . We were ushered onto the grounds of St. Elizabeth's Hospital by guards, who pointed the way. Pound, that sunny afternoon, was surrounded by minions from Catholic University and by members of the *Square Dollar Press* mob. The assembled glares and silences were more than enough to cause us to blush and retreat backwards out of view. Dorothy Pound had whispered: you must realize that he does not admit people who are friendly with that Charles Olson person . . . True, Pound had been quoted in one of the house organs of the sodality as offering John Casper a particularly sage piece of advice as he headed into the South to make mischief in Clinton, Tennessee: "STAY AWAY FROM KIKES & OLSON!"

Neither of these two footnotes to literary history in Farmville, Virginia and Anacostia, Maryland makes very pleasant reading but indicate that the Muse gets stuck in the mire like everybody else in swampy times. I can report, a little more happily, that ten years later Ezra Pound, in Venice, did break his silence towards me. Olson he remembered only as "that large man who never paid any attention to what I said." The Jews were no longer hiding in the forsythia bushes ready to potshot him. He was glad to hear that my bring-em-back-alive tracking of Mina Loy and Basil Bunting had not been wild goose chases and that books and poems had been the result.

Looking at the sunset sky over the Carolina Piedmont this February evening in 1973, I wonder whether even Kenneth Rexroth knows what has happened to Raymond E. F. Larsson; or to Sanders Russell—two authentic caitiffs of our Literary Badlands. And who can tell me the name of that poet, a lapsed Mormon, who wrote the homo-erotic poems about

110

cowboys riding the trail through visionary landscapes? He was later the mayor of a one-horse cowtown in southern Arizona. Robert Lowell? No, that's not it. Not the guy who wrote the *Loon Trilogy* either. It's maybe time we all hit the Trail of Tears, pardners.

*(* Parnassus: Poetry in Review, *Spring/Summer 1973, Vol. 1, No. 2)*

# LETTER TO THE EDITOR
# OF THE SPECTATOR

Dear Sir,

God's teeth! Cor blimey! Sadie, bar the door!—the imperious, supercilious, stiff-lipped Brit-Literati are at it again. They now are spiffing at "the poet Zukofsky," described by Mr. David Wright in *The Spectator* (Oct. 17th) as a "dead-end experimentalist." In one of the Sunday papers, Mr. Anthony Burgess considered it withering and simple enough to call him "a New Yorker, a Communist, a Jew, and a poet" (I think in that order), and expressed doubt that True Poundians would know who this person was. It is now 50 years since EP's *Guide to Kulchur* was dedicated to Louis Zukofsky and Basil Bunting, "strugglers in the desert." The desert is drier than ever, pal. At times like this, I particularly miss evenings with the late Basil Bunting, who would sip a dram or two of the Scottish *aqua vitae* and laugh loudly at such stuff. Unless such writers as Bunting, Ian Hamilton Finlay, and Eric Mottram, on this side of the water, are dolts; and William Carlos Williams, Hugh Kenner, Kenneth Rexroth, Robert Duncan, Robert Creeley, Lorine Niedecker, and Guy Davenport are merely colonial fools, Louis Zukofsky is one of the most astonishing, occasionally matchless, truly virtuoso stylists of recent times. A country boy like myself felt especially honored to publish two of his books.

London/NYC, Oxbridge/Ivy League take care of their own coteries—there's little room for Old Zuk, who earned his bread teaching budding engineers at Brooklyn Polytechnic Institute how to write simple, declarative sentences for their *curricula vitae*. I often take glum comfort in imagining what one of my slit-eyed Anglo-Saxon neighbors in the Blue Ridge mountains of North Carolina would say if he went into the town hall of the village of Scaly Mountain to hear the piano being played by one Vladimir Horowitz. It would be (horrifyingly enough) something like: "Shucks, he's just some old Jew boy from up North. He cain't even play 'The Great Speckled Bird'!"

A little more *bonhomie* and Glenfiddich amongst poets would not be amiss. So, perhaps I am exhibiting a knee-jerk-American over-reaction to Mr. Wright's first-ball dismissal of one of the USA's more interesting poetic figures? Perhaps he (and Mr. Burgess) did not even think they were being unkind to this alien, who wrote in an alien tongue? *I wonder*, as Ronald Firbank said constantly. Louis Zukofsky insisted that the function of poetry was to "record & elate"—it has seldom been said better.

*(October 26, 1987)*

**113**

# THE JARGON SOCIETY

*Jonathan C. Williams Interviews J. Chamberlain Williams*

**JCW:** *Basic stuff for starters. How long has the Jargon Society been operating? And why the name?*

**jcw:** The first publication was a poem of mine with an absolutely hideous title in the Kenneth Patchen mode: "Garbage Litters the Iron Face of the Sun's Child." Lawdy, Lawdy, Miss Clawdy! Patchen could (sometimes) get away with such stuff—let his sycophants beware. The engraver Dave Ruff, whom I had known at Bill Hayter's *Atelier 17* in Greenwich Village, printed one of his copper plates intaglio on this little folded yellow sheet. It was dedicated to Kenneth Rexroth in honor of a fine Chinese meal in North Beach, San Francisco, we all enjoyed. The date was June 1951.

Why the Jargon Society? The word was suggested by the painter Paul Ellsworth, with whom I'd become friendly at the Institute of Design in Chicago earlier that year. The irony of the word appealed. And in French it means "a twittering of birds." It has certainly been that. And, too, a French diminutive, *jargonelle*, refers to a variety of spring pear. Nice to think about.

**JCW:** *A lot of people think Jargon began at Black Mountain College.*

**jcw:** Not true, as I have just indicated; but it *continued* at Black Mountain in July 1951. I went there to study photography with Harry Callahan and

**114**

Aaron Siskind. Emerson Woelffer had told me in Colorado Springs, in June, to watch out for his large friend, Charles Olson, at Black Mountain College. Charles had written a very interesting Melville study, *Call Me Ishmael*, and was quite a guy. I'd never heard of him, but from the moment I spied him having lunch with Ben Shahn in the dining room at the College, he became the energizer, the man who taught me the importance of the writer's press, a self-initiating process that could let you do what you wanted to in the aesthetic realm. "**EACH MAN IS HIS OWN INSTRUMENT!**" Olson sang out.

**JCW:** *What was it with Olson? His size? His blarney?*

**jcw:** I don't "know," but whatever it was, I found him an enchanting 6'8" citizen, a person capable of enkindling others like no one I had ever known. His thinking was a stew-pot of everything: Pound, Dewey, Whitehead. He preached **MAKE IT NEW! ... DO IT YOURSELF! ... BE ROMANTIC, BE PASSIONATE, BE IMAGINATIVE, AND NEVER BE RUSHED!** No one had ever told me things like that at docile Princeton.

**JCW:** *Plunging from Princeton University to Black Mountain College must be one of the stranger career moves in American literary life. How did it come about?*

**jcw:** Too long a tale to tell, and I am merely the person living the life—I probably don't have the clarity to see what "really" happened. My Georgia/North Carolina parents, like all parents from decent working backgrounds and modest educations, wanted me to have better than that. I spent six years at a good prep school (St. Albans at the National Cathedral in Washington, D.C.) and was particularly lucky in having one amazing teacher (John Claiborne Davis) who knew what kindling to use to fire the imaginations of those few of his charges who had imaginations. What worked for me was: Sibelius, Delius, Aldous Huxley, C. S. Lewis, Sorokin, H. P. Lovecraft, Henry Miller, Kenneth Patchen, Redon, Courbet. By the time I got to Princeton, Blake and Rouault had joined this pantheon. Word and image, how to put them together, how to print and publish—it all began to heat slowly on the back burner. Then I met

Patchen, Rexroth, and Miller. I read the anarchist/pacifist literature. And I turned away from the Establishment World of Princeton. Clearly I did not want to become a Byzantinist in the basement of the Morgan Library; or an art critic for the *New Yorker*. Nor did I want to live in the world of competitive business. A great blow to my baffled, conservative, helpful, Southern parents. (More blows were to follow: becoming a poet, becoming a conscientious objector, having male companions in life. "*Oi veh, oi veh, that's all I need,*" sayeth the Despairing Parents. Can you blame them?)

**JCW:** *So, with Olson's precepts ringing in the air of Buncombe County, North Carolina, you began producing artists' books.*

jcw: Yes. Summer 1951 at Black Mountain found people like Fielding Dawson, Joel Oppenheimer, Francine du Plessix, Dan Rice, Mary Fitton, Joe Fiore, Victor Kalos, Nick Cernovich, Edward Dorn, Robert Rauschenberg, Cy Twombly, and me on the premises. Jargon #2 was a poem of Oppenheimer's, "The Dancer," with a drawing by Rauschenberg (the first Rauschenberg used in a publication). It was dedicated to Katherine Litz, who was there that summer teaching. Next, *Red/Gray*, poems of mine, drawings by Paul Ellsworth; next, *The Double-Backed Beast,* Victor Kalos's poems, Dan Rice's drawings. Then two things happened: I went into the Medical Corps (Army) and off to Stuttgart for eighteen months; and I was left $1500 in the will of a friend from Demorest, Georgia, named Charles Neal. In my mind, I had three choices: (1) buy a Porsche automobile; (2) buy a Max Beckmann portrait; (3) start publishing books. Idiotic from the beginning, I opted for #3 and have been an aristocratic, cranky art-beggar ever since.

**JCW:** *Now came actual books instead of pamphlets and broadsides, right?*

jcw: Yes. *The Maximus Poems/1–10,* by Charles Olson; *Fables & Other Little Tales*, by Kenneth Patchen; *The Immoral Proposition,* by Robert Creeley; *Four Stoppages,* poems by myself. The Olson was marvelously printed by the printshop of Dr. Walter Cantz. I had seen examples of their work for New Directions, especially *Sleep in a Nest of Flames*, by Charles

Henri Ford. The offices were within a ten-minute walk from the Fifth General Hospital I was stationed at in Bad Cannstatt. The Patchen was printed in Karlsruhe/Durlach by Tron Brothers, another excellent firm of craftsmen. I learned a lot in a hurry from these two printers. The Creeley (also Tron Brothers) was designed as a little "Japanese" book for the table, with string binding and drawings in the Sumi manner by the Frenchman René Laubiès, painter and translator of Ezra Pound. My poems (Ernst Klett, printer) were also done in an oriental style as a four-part folding paper screen for the table, or to be pinned on the wall. The drawings were by Charles Oscar (the husband of Katherine Litz), who was later murdered on a New York rooftop by some lethal hustler. I remember that there were 200 copies of *Four Stoppages*. It came in a white envelope with my military address imprinted. The price was 50 cents a copy. At a book auction in New York City last spring, James Jaffe, Bookseller, of Haverford, Pennsylvania, paid $1400 for the copy that had belonged to Kenneth Patchen. Since I gave that copy to Patchen in the first place and had to pay the airmail postage to the States, my return on the investment is even less than nothing. Which is not to snarl at dealers and collectors. They play different games in that ball park than I do, but it's comforting to recognize the existence of new fans. Just yesterday, out of the blue came catalog nine from Origin Books (Steven Clay, Merce Dostale, 821 West 43 Street, Minneapolis, Minnesota 55409), 473 items by Jargon Society and writers published by us. A complete surprise.

**JCW:** *Is there any "why" you have published what you have?*

**jcw:** For *pleasure,* surely. I am stubborn, mountaineer Celt with an orphic, priapic, sybaritic streak that must have come to me, along with H. P. Lovecraft, from Outer Cosmic Infinity. Or maybe Flash Gordon brought it from Mongo? Jargon has allowed me to fill my shelves with books I cared for as passionately as I cared for the beloved books of childhood— which I still have: *Oz, The Hobbit, The Wind in the Willows, Dr. Doolittle,* Ransome, Kipling, et al.

Let me quote some of a statement I wrote for Jargon's catalog in 1983:

The Jargon Society has been "at it" for thirty-two years. Jonathan Williams is director and Thomas Meyer is his assistant. Despite the fact that we edit at Highlands, North Carolina (winter/spring), and Dentdale, Cumbria (summer/autumn), we are not ruralist or retreatist by nature. We are elitist in the tradition of James Laughlin's New Directions. We publish the best we know to please ourselves and our friends, and to confound our enemies. Our board includes distinguished Americans: R. Buckminster Fuller, Donald B. Anderson, J. M. Edelstein, and R. Philip Hanes, Jr. Among our friends and advisors are Guy Davenport, Basil Bunting, R. B. Kitaj, Theodore Wilentz, W. H. Ferry, Lou Harrison, and John Russell.

Publication costs for the Jargon Society are underwritten by foundations, corporations, and individuals who support our effort to publish work by poets, writers, photographers, and artists who have the goods to put on the table when the establishment world seems long out to lunch. For yearly contributions of $100 or more, contributors will receive Jargon Society titles as they are published. For contributions of $1000 or more, contributors will be deemed National Patrons and recognized by name on the colophons of forthcoming publications. Contributors of less than $100 may select one current or forthcoming title as a token of our appreciation.

The Republic has never been teeming with readers of real books, *Readers Digest* and *Penthouse Forum* to the contrary. Our sales indicate we reach about five out of every one million souls! Still, the *New York Times Book Review* has said: "The Jargon Society has come to occupy a special place in our cultural life as patron of the American imagination. But however attractive the books are to look at, and they are justly collector's items, the chief pleasure they afford is the intellectual shock of recognizing an original voice ignored by sanctioned critical opinion." Hugh Kenner has said that Jargon is the "Custodian of Snowflakes," and that Jonathan Williams is "America's truffle-hound of Poetry."

**JCW:** *You seem to have a flawless instinct for spending your time and money on what cannot be "sold."*
jcw: Like the man says, I couldn't sell ice to an eskimo or shit to a fly. We have taken such an adversary position for so long that we are stuck in

some amber-like limbo. A few persons respect this. Most keep silence and ignore the books sedulously. Flaubert once made this comment: "I'm frankly a bourgeois living in seclusion in the country, busy with literature and asking nothing of anyone, not consideration, nor honor, nor esteem. I'd jump into the water to save a good line of poetry or a good sentence of prose from anyone. But, I don't believe, on that account, that humanity has need of me, any more than I have need of it." Still, the trick is: getting the printers paid quickly and fully.

**JCW:** *The list is now nearly one of a hundred titles. Some of the most notable would include Robert Duncan's* Letters; *Louis Zukofsky's* Some Time; *Michael McClure's* Passage *(his first book); Ronald Johnson's* A Line of Poetry, A Row of Trees *(his first book); Paul Metcalf's* Genoa *(and five other prose narratives); Bucky Fuller's* Untitled Epic Poem on the History of Industrialization; *Thomas Meyer's* The Bang Book *(his first book);* The Appalachian Photographs of Doris Ulmann; *Ralph Eugene Meatyard's* The Family Album of Lucybelle Crater; *the Art Sinsabaugh/Sherwood Anderson book of Midwestern photographs and chants; Mina Loy's* The Last Lunar Baedeker; *and the complete writings of Lorine Niedecker,* From This Condensery, *in the press at the moment. Many other titles seem marginal and of the Village-Idiot School. How do you justify them?*

**jcw:** I've always followed Pound's old saw: "I now divide poetry into what I can read and what I cannot." People like Simon Cutts and Thomas A. Clark and Russell Edson and Bob Brown have afforded tremendous pleasure. I am as little interested in coterie as I can possibly be. I do not have lunch with Richard Howard four times a week in Manhattan to hear who's hot, who the latest bratpacker is, who will win the Bollingen, or be buried alive in the vaults of the American Academy and Institute of Arts & Letters. Princeton was one club, and Black Mountain was another. I made distance from each as quickly as possible. Most of the people we've published despise ninety-five percent of the others we've done —that's probably a very healthy thing. Remember, you're dealing with a hillbilly oligarch, a crank. Whether it's poetry or photography or vision-

**119**

ary folk-art or persons themselves, I love things that are "bright-eyed, non-uppity, autochthonous, wacko, private, isolate, unconventional, unpaved, non-commercial, non-nice, naive, outside, fantastic, sub-aesthetic, home-style and bushy-tailed." I am delighted to have published Alfred Starr Hamilton and not Robert Lowell. The gentleman members of the Century Club will take care of Mr. Lowell. Mr. Hamilton's fate is much more fragile.

**JCW:** *The Southern visionaries seem to occupy more and more of your time.*

**jcw:** True. After thirty-four years I have published *most* of what I want to in poetry. The Niedecker, finally coming, will be one of our finest books. Beyond that, I still want to do the *Selected Poems of Mason Jordan Mason*. They have seemed worthy and bizarre and idiosyncratic for all of thirty years. We want to do *Drawings of Truth & Beauty* by Bill Anthony. Robert Hughes sees what they're about—can't 5000 other zany citizens do likewise? We want to do Richard Craven's *Notches Along the Bible-Belt*. He's been at it long enough not to be such a well-kept Tarheel secret. There needs to be a superbly produced, huge book of Art Sinsabaugh's banquet-camera photographs. And perhaps another book or two by Simon Cutts. I do not keep up properly with the younger generations. Some of them are nice to look at, as Petronius might say, but they seem to have little to offer but youth. The writing seems untalented. Which cannot be entirely true. It is up to young publishers to convince us otherwise. Anyways, now I write books about weirds, and long walks, and still enough poems to keep my hand in. People don't really like fifty-five-year-old poets any more than they like to drive cars with 55,000 miles. The voice of the bulldozer, not the turtle, is loud upon the land.

**JCW:** *You sound like the aging scold very far from the gadfly-bitten hunkers of the maddening crowd.*

**jcw:** As far as I can get, but that's not all that far these days. Our place, near Highlands, North Carolina, is halfway between Sky Valley, Eastern America's most Southern artificial ski-slope, and a new development called Wild River Condominiums. In simpler times, Sky Valley was just Mud Creek; and the water below the townhouses was Middle Creek. (Observe, please, the poetry of top-dollar land-over-use-cum-ruination.)

I live in hiding from the Cornbelt Metaphysicals, the Alley-Oopists, the Language Poets, the Great Unwashed, the Jewish Princes, the Ivy-League Heavies, the International Homosexual Conspiracy, the Heap-Big He-Men, the Hem & Haw Femmes, the Primal-Scream Minorities, and the Tireless Untalented—there are thousands and thousands of these people ready to push you into a tar pit. Like I said before, there are only about 1420 people in these United States who celebrate what we do —and what anybody else does. We are trying to do a decent job for one and all of these folk. From the rest I hide, like any good hyperliterate rattlesnake. And I beg: **DON'T TREAD ON ME!**

**JCW:** *Does the fact of being "Southern" make any difference?*

**jcw:** I "have no idea" how to answer questions like that. It says on a piece of paper in the courthouse that I was born 8 March 1929 in Asheville, Buncombe County, North Carolina. That means whatever I, and others, make of it. The South produces Jerry and Jesse and Strom; and Thelonious Sphere Monk and Doc Watson, and Clarence John Laughlin (R.I.P.).

It occurs to me that a blurb I recently wrote (not used) for Duke University Press's new edition of my *Blues & Roots/Rue & Bluets* might just give a new reader a fairly clear picture of what J. Williams, Loco Logo-daedalist, is really all about. It reads:

> Guy Davenport remarks that "JW is in himself a kind of polytechnic institute, trained to write poems as spare, functional, and alive as a blade of grass." Ba goom, I bloody hope so, sez I in my non-Appalachian voice. Professor D. says a lot about my work that makes sense. He tells us that the poems are *peripatetic, cathectic, and paratactic.* He's dead right. But let me put such matters, one hopes, in simpler terms.
>
> Consider this: four men are hiking the Appalachian Trail. The mycologist is the one who knows to look for oaks and apple trees on a north slope

and, hence, for morels. The archaeologist won't have to stub his toe to spot the arrowhead or the pot shard. The ornithologist will laugh like a pileated woodpecker if he thinks he's heard Sutton's Warbler in a place it couldn't be. The poet (the guy who knows how to put all the right syllables in their proper places) is the one who wants to stop with the local boy who is digging ramps on the side of Big Bald Mountain and hear what kind of talk he has in his head.

Poets are forever seeing things, whether Angels in trees, or just things written on the sides of buses like "Jesus Saves & Satisfies. Are You?" Poets are forever hearing things—"always the deathless music!" I like to catch people speaking "poems" who never heard of the word *poet* in their lives. It has been my business, along with others (W. C. Williams, Louis Zukofsky, Lorine Niedecker) to try to raise "the common" to grace; to pay very close attention to the *earthy*. I no more write for "nice" people that I do for "common" ones. I make poems for the people who want them. "He was Southern, and he was a gentleman, but he was not a Southern Gentleman," which is Allen Tate talking about Edgar-Allen-Poe-White-Trash. I sense a tradition there.

*Blues & Roots/Rue & Bluets* is a hoard: the best of what the mountains and I have found out about each other, so far. And a little of the worst as well. The tone ranges from the blade of grass (or hot-shot banjo string) picked by the likes of Mr. Earl Scruggs, to the cello sonorities of Frederick Delius, to occasional glorifications and organ points in the manner of another mountaineer, Uncle Tony Bruckner. For those rare souls who wish to look inside, I counsel: **TAKE CHAIRS, DIGEST YOUR DINNER, SIP THE JUG!**

*(Dictionary of Literary Biography Yearbook: 1984,
edited by Jean W. Ross, Gale Research Company, Detroit, 1985)*

# PAUL POTTS (1911-1990)

Paul Potts should not be allowed to depart from the flensed earth without the telling of a good Paul Potts story. *Flensed* is a favourite adjective of Edward Dahlberg, author of *Bottom Dogs*, the novel that so appalled D. H. Lawrence. Paul Potts once crossed the Atlantic with Dahlberg in the 1930s and never forgot him. They were both *caitiffs*, curs who lived by their wits, and they had a flawless feeling for literary slags—they always bit them on the knees.

The story: during my first sojourn in London (spring 1963), Ronald Johnson and I were living in Barbara Jones's splendid house in Well Walk, Hampstead. We decided to give a party for two American guests, Lawrence Ferlinghetti and Roysce Smith (American Booksellers Association). There were Cuba Libres (rum and coke) for the pro-Castroites, and Bourbon Old Fashioneds for the relatively conservative. Both are lethal cocktails. Most of the guests sat in Barbara's back garden (full of poisonous plants), or on the front steps in the Sunday afternoon sunshine. I can still picture William Burroughs, "El Hombre Invisible," looking like the gray husk of some transgalactic insect.

Memory tells me that most of the following were there: Stevie Smith, Mervyn Peake, Christopher Logue, John Heath-Stubbs, John Wain, Christopher Middleton, R. B. Kitaj, Adrian Berg, Tom Phillips, the The-

**123**

mersons, Pete Brown, Spike Hawkins, Tom Raworth, Peter Russell, Rayner Heppenstall, John Sandoe, Arthur Uphill of Bertram Rota's Bookshop—a true cabinet of curiosities. And, also, Paul Potts.

Noticing the absence of Pottsian rant in all quarters, I went up to the third-floor flat. There he was, passed out on a sofa in his inevitable trench coat and tweed flat hat. Stuffed carelessly in his pockets were all of my rare, signed Burroughs first editions. I carefully extricated these, hid them, and left Paul to snooze on. An hour later he came out of the front door, complaining bitterly, "Some bastard's stolen all my bloody books!" At the end of the party, he asked us to take him to supper. And, after that, asked us for the loan of a tenner. How could anyone refuse such sublime chutzpah?

Over the years one imagines the refusals mounted up and up and one heard less and less of the Scourge of Islington. In the past decade very few could give any answer to the question "How's Paul Potts getting along?" Those few who never turned their backs on this poor literary relation deserve to be named: Ray Gosling, the Fentons of Ebberston Hall, Charles Graham of Tuba Press, and Merilyn Thorold. Two lines of his belong on Paul's tombstone:

## IF YOU'RE WALKING TO THE MOON
## I'VE GOT CLEAN SOX FOR YOU

*(* The Independent, *London, September 7, 1990)*

# HENRI CARTIER-BRESSON SAYS THAT "PHOTOGRAPHY IS PRESSING A TRIGGER, BRINGING YOUR FINGER DOWN AT THE RIGHT MOMENT"

**B**ack in the days of Harry Truman, summer of 1951, I arrived at Black Mountain College to study photography with Harry Callahan and Aaron Siskind. Emerson Woelffer, the painter, had told me a few weeks earlier in Colorado Springs to be sure to look up his good pal, Charles Olson, the Big O. It wasn't hard to find Charles by the shores of Lake Eden, the tallest poet one has ever seen or heard of: 6'8", at least. I studied with him as well, and he quickly pushed the right buttons to turn me into a writer and publisher. GO, O!!! Looking at my photo of Olson, and the one of Francine du Plessix and Joel Oppenheimer, indicates that after six weeks using the Rolleiflex, I was as good as I was going to get. (Harry Callahan, a master, said the same thing about himself.) I really don't know what this says about photography, or about me, but a master I ain't. Whatever, I have taken hundreds of black and white negatives over the years and here are a few of them. Mostly I have shot (lacking a darkroom) lots of color film and presented slide shows all over the place—in dire academic groves, art centers, libraries, living rooms, et al. These battered, scratched, faded transparencies are now being digitized and the good news is that David R. Godine is publishing a book of 80 of them, titled *A Palpable Elysium*. Robert Duncan looks better in 2000 than he did in the slide from 1954. Happily, this cannot be said of Jesse

**125**

Helms and Strom Thurmond (sedulously unphotographed by me), but the miserable fact is that they still serve in the Senate of the United States of America, mirabile dictu. They don't read no Duncan and they don't do no good.

If Michel Eyquem de Montaigne had used a Rolleiflex, he would have made essays with it. So, here's one. Voilà!

Charles Olson, Black Mountain College, Black Mountain,
North Carolina, writing *The Maximus Poems*, summer 1951

First exhibition of *The Maximus Poems 1–10*, Galerie Valentien,
Schlossplatz, Stuttgart, Germany, autumn 1953

"Beauty and the Beast." Francine du Plessix and Joel Oppenheimer,
Black Mountain College, North Carolina, 1951

PFC Jonathan Williams, Army Medical Corps, Holderlin's Tower,
Tübingen, Germany, 1953  *Photograph by William Pease*

Toxaway, Transylvania County, North Carolina, 1954

Toxaway, Transylvania County, North Carolina, 1954

Kenneth Patchen (with his cat, Mr. Sitwell), San Francisco, 1954

Robert Duncan, pulling a face, San Francisco, 1955

Kenneth Rexroth, San Francisco, 1955

"Portrait of the Artist as a Spanish Assassin." Robert Creeley,
Black Mountain College, Black Mountain, North Carolina, 1955

WILLIAM C. WILLIAMS M. D.
9 RIDGE ROAD
RUTHERFORD, N. J.

Sept. 8/56

Dear Williams:

        Don't let the "glum days" get you,
I for one would feel lost without the genius of
your publications. It's a strange thing about
"the new", in which category I place what you do,
at first it shocks, even repels, such a man as
myself but in a few days, or a month or a year
we rush to it drooling at the mouth as if it
were a fruit an apple in winter.  Whatever it
is you publish everything is not successful. BUT
to get and not miss the rare excellence that is
a chance that has to be taken. What you are doing
is tremendously important to me. I don't swallow
everything I see even of what I see of yours but
in it or among it I get what I cant get otherwise.

        Use what you like of what I wrote
about DEATH OF 100 Whales and be sure you
sent a copy of the broadside. The finest thing
about you, and not the only thing, is the topography,
the entire appearance of what you print, it is
distinguised and attractive. Nuff said.

                        Sincerely yours

                        Williams

Carl Ruggles, Arlington, Vermont, 1960

Ronald Johnson, Men-an-Tol Stone, Cornwall, England, 1965

Ian Hamilton Finlay, Stonypath, Dunsyre, Lanarkshire, Scotland, 1966

Thomas Meyer, Crockaloyne Bridge, Lune Valley, Cumbria, England, 1977

"Poetic Advice on His 80th Birthday." Basil Bunting,
Rawthey Bridge, Millthrop, Sedbergh, Cumbria, England, 1980

James Laughlin, "Meadow House," Norfolk, Connecticut, 1986

# AND THE RUNNING BLUEBERRY
# WOULD ADORN
# THE PARLOURS OF HEAVEN

The title is Whitman, and almost too good to be true. Kindly make a multiple image in your camera mind of the Good Gray Poet and H. Callahan, Michigan Isolato.

Harry has been clever enough for 42 years to say very little about his art. Self-revelation is dangerous. Who can quite feel the same about Colonel Harland Sanders after noting his cosmic utterance: "Wine tastes like gasoline."? A poet, however, is inclined to say all or nothing. On my wall I have an inscription by Yoshida Kenko: "It is a fine thing when a man who thoroughly understands a subject is unwilling to open his mouth." Never mind whether Yoshida Kenko is the manager of the Kentucky-Fried Chicken franchise in Kyoto or an ancient sage of that tradition which produced Hokusai, William Carlos Williams, Edward Hopper, Louis Sullivan, the Trappist fathers, and Harry Callahan.

Of course the "truth" is: I am much closer to Thomas Wright "Fats" Waller than I am to Kenko. *One never know, do one?* said Fats. I know just about enough to know I never understand a subject thoroughly. I wrote about Callahan twenty years ago in a little book called *The Multiple Image*. There is no copy here on the shelves. I am audacious enough to write again because all my poetic life I have believed totally in a line of Robert Duncan's: "*Responsibility* is to keep the ability to respond."

**143**

Callahan said to me one time: "There are some guys who don't think I understand what I've done. The odd thing is, *I've done it*. If you know what you're searching and looking for, you know what you're doing." Selah.

Poets are the bane of the sober and righteous. They are idiots and nuts just like photographers, and equally wary of writing down words like *chthonic, hagiographic*, and *decontextualization*, even though they know approximately what they mean. Good scholars and critics have written about Callahan, and have done it honorably, unlike ragtag critic-asters, who, like fish, bite at anything, thinking themselves to be more rational than automatic. J. Williams, proudly and obviously daft as a brush, has other fish to fry.

If you write about Callahan, try to give the gentle reader some simple joy, of the kind his photographs are about. We learned long ago from Louis Zukofsky (I quote this over and over) that the purpose of photography, like that of poetry, is: *to record and elate*. Callahan has always taught that too. I went to Black Mountain College in order to study with him and Siskind back in 1951. I learned a little (my fault) about the camera and the darkroom, learned a lot about the companionable drinking of beer, and met a large man named Charles Olson who knocked me silly and turned me into the kind of poet I am.

Now, I'll turn Callahan into some kind of poet, using his collage technique and what I can see and hear "out there." The one poet he talks about is Walt Whitman. He's the one he *understands*. And why is that? The first six lines of *Leaves of Grass* there on page one give us part of the answer:

> One's-self I sing, a simple separate person,
> Yet utter the word Democratic, the word En-Masse.
>
> Of Physiology from top to toe I sing,
> Not physiognomy alone nor brain is worthy for the Muse.
> I say the Form complete is worthier far
> The Female equally with the Male I sing.

And in the beginning pages of "Song of Myself" the clues continue to build: "I lean and loafe at my ease observing a spear of summer grass . . ." "I, now thirty-seven years old in perfect health begin, Hoping to cease not till death . . ." "I am made for it to be in contact with me . . ." "The play of shine and shade on the trees as the supple boughs wag, The delight alone or in the rush of streets, or along the fields and hill-sides, The feeling of health, the full-moon trill, the song of me rising from bed and meeting the sun . . ." "I have instant conductors all over me whether I pass or stop. They seize every object and lead it harmlessly through me. I merely stir, press, feel with my fingers, and am happy. To touch my person to some one else's is about as much as I can stand . . ."

Harry Callahan, poet. I have an image of him in the guise of the splendid Basho, travelling light, with Leica, wide-angle Hasselblad, and single-reflex Rollei, leaving Edo in the spring of 1689. In his white, open-neck shirt he begins his *Narrow Road to the Deep North* also looking a bit like that much later walker, Walter Whitman of Paumanok. Days later he reaches the post town of Sukawa, visits the poet Tokyu, and a priest living in seclusion under a large chestnut tree on the outskirts. He dutifully photographs the sacred tree, writes in his familiar fashion "to say more about the shrine would be to violate its holiness," and pens a brief homage:

> The chestnut by the eaves
> In magnificent bloom
> Passes unnoticed
> By the men of this world.

And then blessed by the bright clouds of unknowing, he lets his mind drift:

> Michigan, 1912,
> my parents were farmers
>
> no art, but
> father liked music:
> Caruso records

■

I got a Rolleicord,
I had no idea,
I got a big bang out of it,
I was nuts about it
except I got it all wrong

■

no background, no formal training
made me uneasy,
but not with photography

■

Ansel, that's what did it—
no monkey business,
all beautifully sharp,

it totally freed me

■

no cropping after Adams,
it's all in the camera

■

I was free to go out
and just look

and photograph
what I wanted to

I loved the number of lines

■

keep the camera in the same place
and show the changes

**146**

tilt it,
if it looked right

■

all my ideas happened in two years . . .
I just keep going back

some were better at first,
some look better now

■

*Leaves of Grass,*
the idea of working that one book
with original ideas from long ago

on the beach,
on the street,
multiples,
people's faces

I'd rather photograph women than men

■

I felt strongly about Detroit;

In Estes Park
I carried an 8 × 10 camera to the top
of a mountain

I never took a picture with it

■

I really thought I was as good as Stieglitz
I only had about four pictures. . . .

"a certain tenderness," said Stieglitz

■

teaching me how little I knew,
I had to teach to get an education

■

Black Mountain?

the students ate up all the food
the previous winter

■

I never knew what I was doing,
so how come you think you know?

■

I was going to be like Van Gogh:
never to be recognized

and do this great stuff

■

you start with an idea,
but then you get lost on something else,
that's where the big thing happens

■

awhile in the city, awhile in the country,
my wife, my daughter
no clear idea
but I know what I don't want to do any more

sure I'll go back to weeds in the snow

you can take pictures seeing anywhere
you want

the visual comes after living

I don't even know what *visual* is anymore

■

I can't talk about photography,
but go ahead and ask. . . . .

■

I just keep photographing and photographing
until they look right

40,000 negatives
and maybe 800 I like

■

I don't mind photography—
all the dumb stuff—

I have to photograph to find out things,
to photograph my way out,

■

and sometimes it's not so nice,
you don't get out for quite awhile

■

I don't see how anybody
can crit pictures anyway,

but if they write good that's nice

it's a lot nicer
if you can do a little talking

■

I don't have the mentality to make money;

I had a lot of fun making these photographs—
that's what's wrong with me

■

drinking and listening to music—

how do you explain that?

the less you have to think
the better

■

I go out on a day
and accept it

I don't think that would have been
a good picture printed right

■

France?

everything was so damned picturesque
it seemed you couldn't possibly
make a picture

in Providence

that house is behind this house
where there should be an alley

■

it's unique because it's you

every person is really very strange,
if you ever find out about them

■

I'm as good as I am now;
I started, and continued

■

I just hope for some positive feeling

anytime you get something that's any good,
it's a surprise

■

when I was here, these trees
meant a lot to me

■

there are "wishes" all the time
when you're doing this

■

I get up in the morning and I say:
maybe I'll take the wide-angle lens

■

an hour's walk
means a lot

you're walking a year later and all of a sudden
you see how it could work

■

in the desert
I thought about Weston
and about
what he must have thought

■

some talk about
Far Eastern Thought;

I guess mine's
Mid-Western

**151**

■

they're all
on the sly

I've always
sneaked about

■

it worked here
as a result of that

■

just enough ideas
to keep doing them

I just keep hoping I can find
more things to do

■

you know, I think I could look forever,
as long as I can see

■

you never know what part of the role
the picture's going to be

■

meeting Eleanor, knowing her,
marrying her—great;

■

the child—great;
photography—great;

learning, getting into teaching
and stumbling through that;
the travel. . . .

those are the things

■

when I went there, it was with my heart
and I felt that they came with their hearts

Forty-four simplicities (more than a roll), snapped from the mouth of a photographer aged 64 at the time. Most of them come from eight tapes made in February and March, 1977, in an interview between Callahan and Harold Jones and Terry Pitts at the *Center for Creative Photography*, the University of Arizona at Tucson. My thanks to the three of them for letting me eavesdrop.

A book of color reproductions follows. None of us has ever seen very many of them because most previously existed only as Kodachrome transparencies. Lou Kahn once said: "The sun never knew how great it was till it struck the side of a building." Harry Callahan was often there to capture it for the rest of us in these, his private vehicles for seeing.

*(Introduction to* Harry Callahan: Color,
*Matrix Publications, Providence, Rhode Island, 1980)*

# JOEL OPPENHEIMER (1930-1988)

Few in Britain will know the name or the poetry of Joel Oppenheimer. He died yesterday, October 11th, amongst the New England maple trees, 58 years old, after a long bout with cancer. Nobody knows who the poets are in such coarse literary times, and, unless a man remains invisible and unknown, I have the gravest doubts about his abilities. His mentors were William Carlos Williams and Charles Olson, i.e., "anti-poets" to America's Eastern Establishment and to the Oxbridge/SW3-NW3 crowd in London.

Back in 1951, the year the Jargon Society first published Joel (with a drawing by another student at Black Mountain College named Bob Rauschenberg), he was busy consolidating his reputation as the slowest softball pitcher in BMC history. He was fun to publish, and he was easy to hit. Which was ok, because he didn't go to pieces and didn't get nasty. Despite many afflictions, remained somehow in one piece (until the onslaught of the final illness), and became, quietly, over the years, one of the few poets to read and re-read. He was a real heart-breaker. (His long poem about chemotherapy, "The Uses of Adversity," must be one of the most harrowing, yet inspiriting, works of our time.)

What a day was chosen for him to die. His beloved New York Mets tied in battle with the Los Angeles Dodgers for the National League baseball playoffs—only one game to go! Joel once wrote a book (*The Wrong Season*) about the joys and horrors of being a Mets fan over the years. One must not forget that poetry and baseball are two of the three best games to play in the soft, sexy grass of Mount Parnassus.

The best account of his life is one he wrote for the flap of the Selected Earlier Poems, *Names & Local Habitations*, which we (the Jargon Society) are about to publish in only a month's time, a book he sadly will never see. He said: "Joel Oppenheimer was born in 1930, educated from 1934–1953; bar mitzvahed in 1943, achieved manhood in 1951. These dates are significant, encompassing a depression, a war, a police action, and the beginnings of the affluent society. He has remained untouched by any of them. He has made poems and children much of his adult life, and also a living. He reads too much, although that's not what made him wear glasses. His penultimate son has a very good swing. He believes love is the *only* game in town, even if it is fixed."

Here is one small early poem, just to indicate his tenderness, his lovely command of what is dismissively called common and ordinary. Nothing was "ordinary" to this mensch of a guy:

### THE LOVER

every time
the same way
wondering when
this when that.
if you were a
plum tree. if you
were a peach
tree.

(The Independent, *London, October 17, 1988*)

# THE MOON POOL AND OTHERS

[This piece was written in the form of a letter to Ian Young in 1979. He was asked by Dennis Cooper, of *Little Caesar* magazine, to guest-edit an issue called "Overlooked & Underrated," which was published eventually in 1981. A decade having passed, it makes sense to re-write and amplify. My friend Gary Knoble was asking just the other day for a compilation of savory texts that the Republican incumbent had never heard of. That's easy. Here it is. JW, July 1989 . . . Addendum, August 1998: Nearly another decade down the drain, so I get to add more titles.]

Dear Ian,

"What a civilization! Nobody even remembers who wrote **THE MOON POOL**." Often I think of that ultimate lament by Kenneth Rexroth. However, good buddy, I remember that Honest Abe Merritt wrote **THE MOON POOL**, and I was very turned on by its unique art-deco, sci-fi eroticism back in the ur-sexy days of Flash Gordon and Batman and Robin. (Gosh all hemlock!—to think that Bruce Wayne was such a conspicuous nob-throb to a generation of panting American adolescents. His thick-as-a-plank side-kick and "ward," Dick Grayson, has probably inherited the penthouse suite and the Batmobile by now and spends a lot of time in the

**156**

leaves on the floor of the Bat Cave with Monica Lewinsky's younger brother, Marvin.)

I'd love to write you a whole book on marvellous caitiff writers who go unread in our dummified times. But, I remain up to my hunkers in chores for the Jargon Society—all that reading and writing that serve to make me internationally unknown, like one had better be these days.

"Of making many books, there is no end." That's in, I believe, *Proverbs* ... "The flesh is sad and I have read all the books." That's Mallarmé. These quotations remind us that each of us has read almost nothing. And why do we read even the little dab that we do? I hope it is for reasons of literary seduction. As the man in the Greek Anthology said so long ago: "WOMEN FOR USE, BOYS FOR PLEASURE, GOATS FOR DELIGHT." Bring on goat-like books!

If you asked the poet Basil Bunting to name the few, world-class masters, he would name you twelve, half of whom you'd never heard of. Viz: Homer, Ferdosi, Manucheri, Dante, Hafez, Malherbe, Aneirin, Heledd, Wyatt, Spenser, Sidney, Wordsworth ... For Basil, that was it. No one in the 20th century, even his great mentor, Ezra Pound, made the Top Dozen.

Who nose from great? as Jimmy Durante used to ask. I know a lot that's "readable" and that will help get a reader through good and bad days and nights. I'll select a few genres and see what I think of, off the top of my head. One thing to mention at the start is that our friend, The Devoted Reader, is going to need the services of a very excellent library system. And then he or she must have civilized sources from which to purchase books. These days the most obliging bookman for used, first-edition, and out-of-print books that I know of in the USA is James Jaffe, PO Box 496, Haverford, PA 19041. Telephone: (610) 649-4221. Another enthusiast is Kevin Rita, *Brickwalk Bookshop,* 966 Farmington Avenue, West Hartford, CT 06019. Telephone: (860) 233-1730. For new books it is useful to establish an account with a shop like *Chapters,* 1512 K Street

NW, Washington, DC 20005. Telephone: (202) 347-5495. The excellent owners are Terri Merz and Robin Diener . . . In England, for new books: *John Sandoe, Books*, 10 Blacklands Terrace, Sloane Square, London SW3 2SP, England (UK). Telephone: (0171) 589-9473. The contact there is Sean Wyse-Jackson. Many of my contacts in the antiquarian book world have retired, so consult a current directory of good shops at a major municipal library.

*Little Caesar* being a more or less specialist magazine, let's start with gay writers. Of those with a "delicate Athenian sensibility," as my friend Marius Bewley used to say, there is the uniquely lucid J. R. Ackerley. The books to read first are **WE THINK THE WORLD OF YOU**, **MY FATHER AND MY-SELF**, and **LETTERS**. His prose style is second to none. When turgidity and the tendency to make too much of what there is out there begin to o'erwhelm me, etc., I sit down and read some Joe Ackerley. Four English novels I have liked lately are **LORD DISMISS US**, by Michael Campbell; **THE SWIMMING-POOL LIBRARY**, by Alan Hollinghurst; **UNNATURAL RELATIONS**, by Mike Seabrook; and the 'odiously funny and delightfully unwholesome' **A ROOM IN CHELSEA SQUARE**, by Michael Nelson. Kevin Esser is a worthy young American writer. **MAD TO BE SAVED** is as good a picture of collegiate life in the seventies as I know. **STREETBOY DREAMS** and **SOMETHING LIKE HAPPINESS** are two other Esser novels to read. And certainly don't overlook a first novel by the young Arkansas writer, Keith Hale: **CLICKING BEAT ON THE BRINK OF NADA**. He already commands much of Ackerley's honesty, intimacy, and ease of style. Real warmth. I call your attention to four more recent novels by excellent craftsmen: **LANDSCAPE: MEMORY**, by Matthew Stadler; **AMERICAN STUDIES**, by Mark Merlis; **THE MAN WHO FELL IN LOVE WITH THE MOON**, by Tom Spanbauer (this is a fantastic book!); and **MYSTERIOUS SKIN**, by Scott Heim.

I undoubtedly show my years and the tastes of my generation when I list the writers I do. *Tant pis.* I like Sissie Writers! So I like very much Ronald Firbank (a sort of Cambridge-trained Mae West), Denton Welch, and Jocelyn Brooke (**THE ORCHID TRILOGY**) . . . As for pedophiles, they mostly

**158**

write so badly they deserve to eat in hell forever at Colonel Sanders' Pluto-Fried-Chicken franchises. Five exceptions: **THE ASBESTOS DIARY**, by Casimir Dukahz (whoever that might be); **SOME BOYS**, by Michael Davidson; **GAME-TEXTS**, by Erskine Lane; **TIME OF OUR DARKNESS** (about an Afrikaner gay teacher and a black kid), by Stephen Gray; and that frank and beautifully composed series of journal entries, **PUPPIES**, by the Californian, John Valentine. I really don't think people like Ed White and David Leavitt are in his class, but, per usual, he lives in a Mendocino coast town and they live where the action is.

As for One-Hand Classix, the genuinely dirty stuff that keeps the polymorphous mind off abominations like Pat Buchanan? **NAKED ON MAIN STREET**, by Richard Amory. (There was even a rumor around in the seventies that RA was really W. H. Auden, the Lord Teeny-Meat, longing for something long. It somehow seems doubtful.) Also, his **LOON TRILOGY** is pretty jolly, particularly if read aloud by three or four lecteurs. Belles-lettrists will roll about on the floor ... Since my tastes run to the rustic pastorale ("Out on the farm we used/butter," to quote a Gavin Dillard poem), I must confess to admiration for five tales to exercise the most jaded of one-eyed trouser-snakes: **LONG TIME COMING**, by Louis Stout; **ALL TIME HARD**, by Charlie Peters; **THE CHRONICLES OF FENWAY ACADEMY**, by Peter Zupp; **THE CHRONICLES OF THE STARCROSS COMPLEX**, by Scott Altman; and **DO MY THING**, by Richard Manbow and Lyn Pederson. Oh, one more: **MY LOVER, MY TEACHER**, by David Rinkler. Who in the world are these elusive, wretchedly paid scriveners? They have warmed the cockles of thousands of gay guys in dire places like Statesville, North Carolina, where only the seamy news stand just off the town square afforded any of the crumbs of erotic literacy.

Childhood writers? If they were marvellous then, they often turn out to be marvellous now. I continue to abide by **OZ**, as written by L. Frank Baum and his three successors. **THE WIND IN THE WILLOWS**, by Kenneth Grahame, is still a wonder. (Try to hear it in the BBC radio version read by David Davies.) Don't miss Kipling's **JUST SO STORIES**; or, **OLD MAN**

**ADAM AN' HIS CHILLUN** and **OLD KING DAVID AN' THE PHILISTINE BOYS**, by Roark Bradford. Or, **UNCLE REMUS**, by Joel Chandler Harris. Something very different: **LILITH** and **PHANTASTES**, by George MacDonald . . . I had enough sense at age 8 to recognize that **THE HOBBIT**, by Professor J. R. R. Tolkien, was well worth the 29 cents it cost me off the remainder-table in Woodward & Lothrop's Department Store in Washington, DC, in 1938. I re-read his mature trilogy, **THE LORD OF THE RINGS**, every three years just to make sure I haven't gone Republican or dead in the head. And then, one mustn't forget Beatrix Potter, Arthur Ransome, E. Nesbitt, Hugh Lofting, Hawthorne, A. A. Milne, and Robert Louis Stevenson. And two recent contenders by Richard Adams: **THE PLAGUE DOGS** and **WATERSHIP DOWN** (which is definitely not **WATERED-DOWN SHIT**, as one wag has it). The best fantasy I have read in years are the first two volumes of a trilogy called **HIS DARK MATERIALS**, by Philip Pullman. They are **THE GOLDEN COMPASS** and **THE SUBTLE KNIFE**. Wonderful writing! I have no idea who wrote Nancy Drew, Tom Swift, Don Sturdy, and The Hardy Boys. But, great stuff for budding WASPs, as were the comic books of those dim-daysofyore.

Mysteries?—another genre despised by word-queens and people who stay too long in the bathroom. Every ten years or so I do jigsaw puzzles for a season and then run through a huge diet of whodunnits. Back in the 1970s I devoured all the Lew Archer novels of the late Ross MacDonald. It could be argued that all he did was write the same book over and over (out of some complex Jungian muddle in which the murderer was always the unknown grandson of the incestuous aunt's cousin's mother, etc.), but he is very stylish. Another American I like is Robert B. Parker and his Boston detective, Spenser ("I spell it like the English poet"). K. C. Constantine (rumored to be the alias of some "really good" novelist) is good enough for me. A great character is his police chief, Mario Balzic. The dialogue is terrific; and how about a title like **THE MAN WHO LIKED SLOW TOMATOES**! Just lately I have run across Jonathan Valin, one of the best of the new breed. Who would have thought a big, butch shamus from Cincinnati named Harry Stoner could be so engaging? Try **THE LIME PIT, DEAD LETTER, DAY OF WRATH**, and **FINAL NOTICE. THE ISAAC QUARTET**, by Jerome Charyn is worth chasing down. And a very tough book called **DANCING BEAR**, by James Crumley.

I am nearly forgetting the excellent Joseph Hansen. He has taken over Raymond Chandler's territory in Southern California and his likeable insurance investigator is big Dave Brandstetter, who happens to be gay but doesn't fret about it. Eight or nine solid books. Hansen wrote in a more unfettered style under the name of James Colton and had to be published by porn merchants: **HANG UP** is very good, and I remember three others named **COCKSURE** and **KNOWN HOMOSEXUAL** and **TODD**. Someone else who's relatively new in the field is Michael Connelly. Three to read are **THE POET, TRUNK MUSIC** and **BLOOD WORK**. Then there are the two richly detailed thrillers set in New York around the turn of the century, **THE ALIENIST** and **THE ANGEL OF DARKNESS**, by Caleb Carr.

The English remain very agile at creating detective fiction. Julian Barnes (of **FLAUBERT'S PARROT**) has written (using the *nom de plume* Dan Cavanaugh) four or five lively mysteries featuring the bilious, bisexual sleuth named Duffy, though he seems more just-plain-gay as the books continue. It is comforting to see that Agatha Christie and Dorothy Sayers have their equals at work at the moment. (Stevie Smith once told me how much she enjoyed reading Agatha Christie in French translations. The sheer pleasure of it all was enhanced by seeing if they'd say "church mouse" or "church rat.") P. D. James is a bit heavy and urbane in the knowing London way, but her poetry-writing policeman, Adam Dalgliesh, is a substantial invention, and James is very good. Even superior, it seems to me, is the remarkable Ruth Rendell, and the great news is there are about 30 books, including two or three written under the alias of Barbara Vine, when she is at her most novelistic and stylish. Many of the books feature Chief Inspector Reg Wexford in a town called Kings Markham, near the Sussex Downs. Very good of their kind. But Rendell is amazing when she simply starts diagramming a plot in which people (often very insane) of very different social orders begin to converge and destroy each other. Uncanny and scary stuff. Try her best one, **A JUDGMENT IN STONE**, in which the horrific murder of a whole family is revealed on page one, and the cause is shown to be a servant's illiteracy, implacably spelled out over the next several hundred pages. Excellent novel writing. **THE KILLING DOLL** is another chiller. A new contender to watch is Minette Waters, whose four or five titles I don't have at hand.

Horror and the Supernatural? Howard Phillips Lovecraft was my transition from boys' adventure books to the surrealism of Henry Miller and Kenneth Patchen. Nothing wrong with a "third class" writer with a peerless imagination. **THE SHADOW OUT OF TIME** and **THE CASE OF CHARLES DEXTER WARD** are perhaps better than I remember. They stick in the conk. Others that do: **THE HOUSE ON THE BORDERLAND**, by William Hope Hodgson; **THE PURPLE CLOUD**, by M. P. Shiel; **THE HILL OF DREAMS**, by Arthur Machen; and a lot by H. G. Wells, Olaf Stapledon, M. R. James, Saki, Lord Dunsany, E. F. Benson, A. E. Coppard, Walter de la Mare, Clark Ashton Smith, Algernon Blackwood, and Colin Wilson. The two current writers of boogieman prose I like best are Stephen King (The World's Richest Writer, who rivals the Big Mac for style and usability) and the more literate Peter Straub. **SALEM'S LOT** and **THE SHINING** are first-class books by Mr. King. And, **IF YOU COULD SEE ME NOW**, **GHOST STORY**, and **MYSTERY** by Mr. Straub. Two other writers of interest: Whitley Strieber (**THE HUNGER, THE WOLFEN**) and Robert R. McCammon (**MYSTERY WALK**). Check your local drugstore.

Letter writers? It's hard to play in the same ballpark with John Keats and Gustave Flaubert, but Oscar Wilde, D. H. Lawrence, and Ezra Pound belong there. I love reading the letters of Edward Lear; the six volumes of the **LITTLETON/HART-DAVIS LETTERS** (published in the UK by John Murray in London); and **THE FARTHEST NORTH OF HUMANNESS** (letters by Percy Grainger). Every letter I received from Lorine Niedecker was a benison.

162

And my correspondence from Guy Davenport, Edward Dahlberg, and Ian Hamilton Finlay will end up in books later on.

Autobiography and Biography: **LOOKING BACK**, by Norman Douglas; **MEMOIRS OF A DISAPPOINTED MAN**, by W. N. P. Barbellion; **RUM, BUM AND CONCERTINA**, by George Melly; **DANTE CALLED YOU BEATRIX**, by Paul Potts; **VOICES**, by Frederic Prokosch; and **BENEATH THE UNDERDOG**, by Charles Mingus . . . Richard Ellmann on Oscar Wilde; Humphrey Carpenter on Auden, Pound, and Tolkien; Gerald Clarke on Truman Capote; Vivian Noakes on Edward Lear; Mark Holloway on Norman Douglas; Victoria Glendinning on Edith Sitwell; John Bird on Percy Grainger; Eric Fenby on Delius; Jan Swafford on Charles Ives; and John Lahr on Joe Orton. Herbert Leibowitz's book on American autobiographies, **FABRICATING LIVES**, is a winner. A recent book by James Lord, **SOME REMARKABLE MEN**, is outstanding.

Travel and Reporters of the Natural World? **THE TRAVELS OF WILLIAM BARTRAM** is one the great 18th-century American books, right up there with Mr. Jefferson. I include it because it has only been re-discovered in the past 50 years. I read anything by John Stewart Collis with attention. This goes for W. H. Hudson, Richard Jeffries, Edgar Anderson, Carl Sauer, and Jaime D'Angulo. **THE DIARIES OF FRANCIS KILVERT** are marvelous. Geoffrey Grigson's **THE ENGLISHMAN'S FLORA** is a source book like no other. As is a huge symposium published by the University of Chicago: **MAN'S ROLE IN CHANGING THE FACE OF THE EARTH**. I am just skimming. If I need to know something specific about my neighbor in the Blue Ridge, the Timber Rattlesnake, I go immediately to Lawrence Klauber's two remarkable volumes . . . I often go to Henry James' **THE AMERICAN SCENE** for insights, as I do to a recent book, **BLUE HIGHWAYS**, by William Least Heat-Moon. What an extraordinary volume. It reminds you that a little bit of America is still here. His second book, **PRAIRYERTH**, sits on the shelf too big to chew on. Two books by Norman Douglas on the Austrian Vorarlberg are classics: **ALONE** and **TOGETHER**; as is **TRAVELS WITH A DONKEY**, Robert Louis Stevenson's account of his trip across the Cévennes. And not to forget two fine accounts of long walks: **A TIME OF GIFTS** (from London to Hungary), by Patrick Leigh Fermor; and **A WALK THROUGH BRITAIN** (from Land's End to John O'Groats), by John Hillaby.

Fiction and Essays? I don't read much of either, but here are books I keep on the shelf and often pick up for another read: **THE GREEN CHILD** and **THE CONTRARY EXPERIENCE**, by Herbert Read; **BLACK SPRING** and **THE BOOKS IN MY LIFE**, by Henry Miller; **THE JOURNAL OF ALBION MOONLIGHT**, by Kenneth Patchen; **IN THE AMERICAN GRAIN**, by William Carlos Williams; **STUDIES IN CLASSIC AMERICAN LITERATURE**, by D. H. Lawrence; **TRACKS IN THE SNOW**, by Ruthven Todd; **BECAUSE I WAS FLESH** and **THE SORROWS OF PRIAPUS**, by Edward Dahlberg; **CALL ME ISHMAEL**, by Charles Olson; **THE TERRITORY AHEAD**, by Wright Morris; **A MORE GOODLY COUNTRY**, by John Sanford; **GENOA**, by Paul Metcalf; **GOING AWAY**, by Clancy Sigal; **LOLITA**, by Vladimir Nabokov; **RIDDLEY WALKER**, by Russell Hoban; **THE NATURAL MAN**, by Ed McClanahan; **THE ALBANY TRILOGY**, by William Kennedy; **THE DEPTFORD TRILOGY**, by Robertson Davies; **AFFLICTION**, by Russell Banks; **OUR SOUTHERN HIGHLANDERS**, by Horace Kephart; **A HANDY GUIDE FOR BEGGARS**, by Vachel Lindsay; and **AMERICAN FRIED**, by Calvin Trillin.

The best novel I have read in years is **ON THE BLACK HILL**, by Bruce Chatwin. Its simple but visionary style evokes both Samuel Palmer and the eye of the Pre-Raphaelites. It seems a more "exotic" book than **IN PATAGONIA**, and it's amazing that Chatwin wasn't born in that part of Wales instead of being from Birmingham, England. I still haven't read his **THE SONGLINES** or **UTZ**. As for essays, Guy Davenport's **THE GEOGRAPHY OF THE IMAGINATION** is in a class by itself. And it is always a pleasure to read around in the prose pieces by Kenneth Rexroth and James Laughlin ... If you can stand the thought of another tale of growing-up-down-South-abused-by-bad-daddy-and-dirtpoor-too, I know of four powerful memoirs: **THE LIARS' CLUB**, by Mary Karr; **BASTARD OUT OF CAROLINA**, by Dorothy Allison; **WINTER BIRDS**, by Jim Grimsley; and **ALL OVER BUT THE SHOUTIN'**, by Rick Bragg ... Wait, I am forgetting a very interesting writer named E. Annie Proulx. She is one tough hombre. Her books are all distinctive and different in kind. Good dialogue, clear diction, and a rich and curious vocabulary. Read **POSTCARDS** (the best); **THE SHIPPING NEWS**; and **ACCORDION CRIMES**.

Academic and Scholarly Books? A Kentucky matron once accosted Guy Davenport at a horsy occasion in the Blue Grass. "Professor Davenport, why you're the most *over-educated* man I've ever met!" I'd give the lady no qualms at all. I'm real strong on sight and sound, dismissive of intellection, and just about as dumb as a three-dollar dog. Abstract ideas know better than to grope me. Still, I have a brief list: **THE POETICS OF SPACE**, by Gaston Bachelard; **THE ORPHIC VOICE**, by Elizabeth Sewell; **LIFE AGAINST DEATH**, by Norman O. Brown; **THE SOCIETY I LIVE IN IS MINE**, by Paul Goodman; **THE LAW OF CIVILIZATION & DECAY**, by Brooks Adams; **HOMO LUDENS**, by Johan Huizinga; **PHALLÓS**, by Thorkil Vanggaard; **CHRISTIANITY, SOCIAL TOLERANCE, AND HOMOSEXUALITY**, by John Boswell; **THE STRUCTURE OF EVERYDAY LIFE**, by Fernand Braudel; **THE POUND ERA**, by Hugh Kenner . . . A little Walter Pater and Walter Benjamin never hurt nobody none. And it doesn't hurt to drag out Pound's **ABC OF READING** and Zukofsky's **A TEST OF POETRY** once a year, to remind oneself what the inestimable values of writing can be at their best.

Books of No Particular Category? The two sports that seem to produce the most memorable writing are cricket and baseball. If one bores you, the other will too, lunkheads! The literary authorities on cricket are Nevil Cardus and John Arlott. Had I not spent 25 years trying to figure this game out, I might have tried to fathom **FINNEGAN'S WAKE**. (I did right.) Baseball, lately, has been beautifully served by Roger Angell and Thomas Boswell. I suppose a life without baseball is still life, but just barely . . . Some cartoonists amaze me, like R. Crumb, with creations like Angelfood McSpade, Captain Pissgums & His Gay Pirates; and the magazine, *Despair Comics*. I also have everything I can find by the ineluctable and ineffable Bernie Kliban; and by my most favorite *luftmensch* of all: Glen Baxter. I mean, we're talking cosmic and kiss my grits if you don't think so. However, from the down-right ridiculous to the demotic sublime, a work that occupies me as much as any is the magisterial **ENGLISH DIALECT DICTIONARY** (6 big tomes), by the self-taught son of a Yorkshire shepherd, the magnificent Joseph Wright. Have a few drams of malt and spend an evening with this *arcanum*. Find out what *triddlings* and *daggle-tails* are, for starters! You're into big doo-doo, to quote the gentleman named Geor-Gebush.

Poetry? Can you not spare us, Good Lord? Poetry lovers like Martial but don't like Horace. They like Archilochos but don't like Sappho and Her Dykes On Bikes! I hesitate to mention even *one* poet, but, of recent ones, I'd hate not to have investigated: Kenneth Rexroth, Kenneth Patchen, Louis Zukofsky, Charles Olson, Robert Duncan, Jack Spicer, James Broughton, Philip Whalen, Ronald Johnson, Alfred Starr Hamilton, Russell Edson, Mason Jordan Mason, James Laughlin, J. V. Cunningham, Lorine Niedecker, Basil Bunting, Stevie Smith, Simon Cutts, Ian Hamilton Finlay, Thomas A. Clark, Thomas Meyer, Joel Oppenheimer, Robert Creeley—"they are pearls that were his eyes!"

A hundred other books have been stupidly overlooked. There's nothing quite like stupidity. Keeps you reglur.

Love,

Jonathan

# COCKTALES TO PLEASE PRIAPUS

priapean is a measure
consisting of a glyconic
and a pherecratean (qqv)
separated by a diaeresis


still gettin whatcha want
yeah but only just


onan in arkansas big
man chokin his chicken


size matters sighs matter


surely the best faux-epitaphe
pour son sepulchre ever
penned is by john
cheever it goes i

never disappointed a hostess
and i never took
it up the butt


i telephoned my old
master at st. albans
school and asked how
he was doing he
said fine i can't
see and i can't
hear and i stumble
about like silenus but
the important thing is
i can still come
and i can still
make other people come
that's the important thing
and well what else
can you really say


here's one i heard
at a party recently
for the boys at
hog river what's better
than roses on a
piano tulips on an
organ yar says reuben


tad tomkins was interviewing
the ineffable andy warhol

and the ineffable one
got in first and
asked do you have
a big cock tomkins
thought he'd asked do
you have a big
clock so he said
not especially and glanced
furtively at his wrist


slip between the sheets
with the topaz man

### DAWN SONG IN THE PENNINE DALES

ee wakey wakey wakey
git hands off snakey

### GAVIN

my dick's too short
to fuck with god


at the senate hearing
senator thurmond then asked
well judge thomas just
how big is it
well said judge thomas
about the size of
two beer cans so
then the senator asked
well clarence is that

**169**

eight ounces or twelve
ounces the american people
need to know facts
they are so deprived
not depraved just deprived

hey the dog's going
to smell your underwear

and now what we
need is a good
joke with which to
remember 1998 a very
singular year in our
tawdry and tacky republic
so what do you
call a blow-job that
lasts for eight days
give up well the
answer is hanukkah lewinsky

can't you write nice
poems about flowers and nature
stuff you mean like
amanita phalloides and stinking
willie sure if that's
really what you want

*(Some of these meta-fours have appeared in several issues of* Oyster Boy Review. *Thanks to Jeffery Beam, Poetry Editor, for permission to reprint.)*

# MAKING THE UNSAID SAY IT ALL

trato himself is frankly homosexual. He writes good and at times pretty verse, but he is, as a rule, quite *terre à terre* and often very gross." A few words from W. R. Paton, who translated Strato's *Musa Puerilis* (or *Mousa Paidike*) in the Loeb Classical Library's edition of *The Greek Anthology*, where it's tucked in as Book XII. (Paton translates all but some twelve poems, which he leaves in the Latin to keep our loins from suffering Attic Up-Lift.)

*The Greek Anthology*, or *Palatine Anthology* (the unique manuscript resides in the Palatine Library at Heidelberg), was compiled by the Byzantine Constantrinus Cephalas in the tenth century. The major source was a Garland by the Gadarene poet Meleager. Strato of Sardis came later and lived during the reign of Hadrian (A.D. 117–138). Sardis, capital of the kingdom of Lydia, is no more, though we must owe to the goings-on there recorded by Strato the existences of such Sardises as those present in Louisiana, Mississippi, North Dakota, Ohio, Pennsylvania, and Tennessee. Who will write the *Musa Puerilis* of Sardis, Louisiana? (Straight-O makes a good cover.)

Tom Meyer spares us the old straight Strato. We get instead imitations, cullings, reworkings, and take-offs—as though all the words to be used in a "translation" were picked up from the debris on the floor and com-

**171**

posed in a new mind. It is obvious that Strato of Sardis did not write so clearly, lovingly, and well as Tom Meyer. He has let the Unsaid say it all. The boys in the poems are not just bits and pieces of Greek marble—they are fleshed out and their sphincters work.

TM: "I arranged them in a sequence which tells the story of an older man who loves boys in general. As the poems proceed one boy begins to emerge, but right when he's there he's got a hair on his leg & beginning to get a beard (i.e., by Strato-convention, no longer a *puer*). Love goes. The poems end with the man loving boys in general. Again. . . . The poems in such sequence give a sad and unloving shape to the kind of false eros that makes men chase boys & boys toy with the hearts of men."

Glamour and Venal Teeny-Bop Beauty continue to un-man too many. Why, right this morning on Plain American Family-Viewing TV ("The Today Show"), Henry Miller, Kindly Ass-Man Grandpa, was jawing with Norman Mailer: "Christ, did you see that boy in the movie of *Death in Venice*? What a boy! I could have fallen for him myself!" "Beware *puer*, Henry. Look what that ice-dolly Tadzio did to poor Dirk Bogarde— made his make-up melt and his heart stop. 'O Love, O love, O Hairless Love . . !' "

I am only getting to Dr. Jung and his minions, but I can hear Marie Louise von Franz going on over the Puer Aeternus at divine Swiss length. "*Ja, ja*—a thing of beauty and a boy forever," she sighs . . .

*Ach*, the dangers are enough to discourage any but the most ardent, committed paedophile from his task.

> Boys
> will be
> boys'

it says in a poem of mine for the dejected Comte Jacques d'Adelsward-Fersen. Over the entrance to his villa on Capri was chiseled in Latin: **AMORI ET DOLORI SACRUM. "SACRED TO LOVE & SADNESS."**

Think how sad the English "Uranian Poets" were, back in the Yellow

Book Days. Gather ye "Bud" Rose while ye may—he'll not even know he's made out of pure, unadulterated thorns until he's sunk them in your mentor's heart and left you fainting and falling. James Hillman writes about the why of all this in a remarkable essay, "Senex and Puer," dated 1967. One does not have to be a Jungian to recognize the insights of these two passages:

> The feeling of distance and coldness, of impermanence, of Don Juan's ithy-phallic sexuality, of homosexuality, can all be seen as derivatives of the *puer*'s privileged archetypal connection with the spirit, which may burn with a blue and ideal fire but in a human relationship may show the icy penis and chilling seed of a satanic incubus.

And: "These *pueri* are only flower-people like Hyacinthus, Narcissus, Crocus, whose tears are but wind-flowers, anemones of the Goddess, and whose blood gives only Adonis-roses and Attis-violets of regret; they are flower-people who are unable to bear the suffering of carrying their own meaning through to the end, and as flowers they must fade before fruit and seed."

Even in the intense linguistic highlight that Tom Meyer plays over these éphebes, there is no neglect of the dark underside—from Strato to right now. Too little love; too much cockteasing. Very hard to expect boys to grow up ever, if men won't.

*(Introduction to* Uranian Roses, *by Thomas Meyer,*
*Catalyst Press, Scarborough, Ontario, 1977)*

**173**

# "THEY CALLED FOR MADDER MUSIC AND FOR STRONGER WINE!"

*(A Note on Reading Poetry—Not Once But Three Times—*
*At North Carolina Wesleyan College, Rocky Mount, NC)*

There is no rocky mount to see when you get to Rocky Mount. There is a sign indicating that Jim Thorpe played semi-pro baseball once upon a time. There is no sign to tell you that Thelonious Sphere Monk was born there, in an alley called Red Row. Red Row used to have a metal signpost, but now that the area has been targeted for Urban Renewal, the signpost has fallen over and been sold for scrap. You may eat at the first-ever Hardee's. You may be slightly astonished by the motel architecture on Highway 301 North. You will be a little disappointed by the barbecue at Bob Melton's famous old place. These days it tastes very dry, and it is chopped fine in a machine. (There is a cryptic sentence in Bob Garner's book on North Carolina barbecue, *Flavored by Time*: ". . . Rocky Mount barbecue has always been chopped finer than that in other cities . . .") Only the hushpuppies seem up to snuff.

For longer than he would like to remember, Professor Leverett T. Smith, Jr. has been preaching the gospel of poetry and sport to cretinous undergraduates at NC Wesleyan. Talk about the *vox clamans in deserto*, Terry Smith has my vote. Most of his charges, who have been exposed to nothing more culturally complex than a Big Mac or a Whopper, could not tell you which is which. Still, the Professor is there to profess and to try to stick something decent in their tiny little minds. He brings poets like Joel Oppenheimer and J. Williams to his colonial-styled campus in the pine woods behind a Jeffersonian serpentine wall along the highway. JW read there one day in November, 1984, in a pleasant space in the library with comfortable seats and good acoustics. He read from *Blues & Roots* and he tried *real hard*. On the next two pages are verbatim transcripts from students. Win one, lose a few . . .

■

—Williams says the pleasure of poetry is to listen very closely and not to think about it.

—The poetry reading was very enjoyable. The library was very packed. I was surprised that what he read was not his own poetry. But the fact that he read about everyday simple stuff that is easily understood.

—I thought that Jonathan Williams was very clever in the way he worded and the way he expressed himself and got his point across. I also liked the way he used his cigar.

—I thought that it was going to be boring at first but I thought that it was really read good. He is an excellent poetry reader. He made it sound like poetry is supposed to sound. Big Blue was an unreal poem.

—I thought the poetry reading by Jonathan Williams was very entertaining. I had never attended a poetry reading before, but I am pleased that I went to this one. It was funny, too. I had anticipated that it would be extremely boring, but it wasn't. I really enjoyed it.

—The poetry reading I felt was excellent. This was the first time I really enjoyed listening to poetry being read. The speaker had a way of making his poems meaningful and understandable. I have come to the conclusion that poetry isn't bad at all.

—I was really pleased with the poetry reading, expecially the facial expressions and tone of voice Jonathan Williams used. Many times, poets are boring when they give readings, but Williams kept my attention from the very beginning. I would like to hear him again in the near future.

—I felt it was very interesting to hear some things about North Carolina and Virginia that I never knew before. The only thing that was hard to do, was to understand his poems because you just had to listen and not think about what he was saying.

—The speaker on poetry was something new to me and I'm sure it was new to others. I thought that the poetry was funny but there was more sex poetry than anything else. Overall, it turn out good. I would go again.

—The poetry reading was the wildest talking thing I have ever heard. I wish that he had another poem about old blue. Some of the words were hard to understand. But all and all it was a good lecture.

—His poetry was very entertaining some of it was a bit off the wall and some I did not expect from a man of his age.

—Jonathan Williams' poetry reading wasn't what I expected. I went there with the feeling of boredom. Thinking it would be the worst thing I've ever heard. Instead it was very enjoyable. All of his poems I could relate to. Most poem and poets for that matter have all of these abstract meanings and I don't know what they're about. But Jonathan Williams' poems were very relaxing and some were very humorous. The tone in his voice was great.

—I really like most of Jonathan Williams' poems. I like the way he said that the meaning is in the sound of the poetry itself being written and I feel very fortunate to have heard it from the poet himself. This gave more meaning to the poetry itself, because he said it the way he meant it.

—Unfortunately I was unable to attend this most prestigious event. I sadly regret this happening. From what I have heard about the readings and lecture it was a magnificent event. My life will not be fully complete because of my missing Jonathan Williams.

*(Unpublished, 1984)*

# APRIL FOOL'S
# IMITATION-TYPE TEST
# TO WHILE AWAY A LITTLE TIME

If you have read the various epistles I have been passing out, been attending class and evening hoe-downs, and digesting slowly the books I have recommended to you, then you might be expected to answer the following questions. Have a go!!!

(1) In tracing the background of Ragtime, I stressed two composers with French backgrounds (one frog, one cajun), and one black pianist from Texarkana, Arkansas. Who are they? Please spell them correctly.

(2) Ezra Pound and Louis Zukofsky concur that the pleasures of poetry are *three*. I.e., they are the supreme qualities of what three faculties brought to bear upon the words?

(3) What has President Nixon brought us?

(4) What Japanese haiku-master wrote a travel journal which can be considered *indispensable* to all poets, particularly those studying with Jonathan Williams this very month?

(5) What are your five favorite architectural structures, or landscapes, or wilderness areas?

(6) What drunkard's last half-dollar climbs, with how sad feet, the sky over town?

(7) List 10 poems that stick in your head. From Homer on down. If you

can't remember the names of 10 favorite poems, then we are wasting our time . . .

(8) What does the title *An Ear in Bartram's Tree* mean?

(9) What spring flowers (or birds or flowering trees) have given you pleasure recently? Name at least ten. Use local names, not scientific ones, when you can.

(10) Why did you not come to see the films of James Broughton or hear him read his poems? One student said he didn't like to be *intimidated* by people from the outside—an honest answer, if a deplorable one. I do not take poetry *casually*; I admit to being bemused by people who do, and I am always interested in such ticklish matters. (I sometimes think that the students in Winston are spoon-fed, much too comfortable, and more than a little vague. I have been known to be wrong . . . ) The School of the Arts, Wake Forest, Reynolda House, and I spent $500 to bring him here; and Mr. Broughton travelled hundreds of miles for the occasion. The arts are a community and we owe each other attention, especially when we are as accomplished as JB.*

(11) I have said on many occasions that a course in reading and writing could perhaps be better taught as *manners* or *decorum*. I.e., that craft, in large part, consists of being receptive, democratic, ecological and in not thinking that the world rises and sets in our own private anal orifice. Do you agree? More particularly, do you see that *poetry* can sometimes be

---

*Those who did not come to Trap Hill today, Sunday, April 1st, for the centenary celebration of Sergei Vassilievich Rachmaninov (1873–1973) missed a very fine afternoon of music, beer, and warm, sunny weather—the Lewis's waterfall was at its best. You got no chill at all after swimming because the wind was warm. The only people who accepted my invitation were friends from Penland School, who had to drive 3 hours (one way) up the Blue Ridge Parkway from Spruce Pine. This occasion assures me that it is silly to schedule any more such events for the benefit of Laodicean & Midianite students with an advanced case of the Mississippi-Fat-Ass. The hike on the Appalachian Trail (April 14–15) may be enjoyed by whomever, but don't ask me a thing about it. Find Mt. Rogers, Virginia for yourself. Nothing in life is more dangerous in life than expressing, or expecting, enthusiasm.

the making of refined art *objects,* not simply forms of therapy, self-expression and gunning for people?

(12) Bucky Fuller says: "The possibility of the good life for any man depends on the possibility of realizing it for all men. And this is a function of society's ability to turn the energies of the universe to human advantage."

Buck Johnson says: "Music is to make people happy!"

Francis Bacon says he wants: ". . . to make the mind of men, by the help of art, a match for the nature of things."

Comment, very briefly, on one of these three; or, give us your own basic definition of why poetry is worth writing and reading.

(13) Baker's-Dozen Question: Just what does Mae West mean when she says: "Use what's lyin' around the house!"?

If the 13 questions strike you as preposterous or silly or hopeless, then either you haven't been paying attention or I have been assuming you were capable of study without being belabored and yelled at. I am certainly willing to take some of the *blame,* since I lead my life among people who are working artists and not people at the beginning of careers, with various vague ambitions, whims, fancies, etc. You can write me a paper on this subject if you care to. I like cards face-up, on the table . . . If you get through this period of three or four months and feel more *encouraged* than discouraged, that is actually quite a lot. If poetry just isn't worth it to you, then by all means get a job selling tires, insurance, or Judo & Karate for Christ. Orpheus will respect your decision.

*(JW gave this test to his Wake Forest University students, April 2nd, 1973)*

# THE POETRY OF WORK

*Which is Subtitled for Some Strange Reason:*
*And Two Little Pigs (Arty & Crafty) Went to Market*

To invite a poet to a conference is like asking Banquo's ghost to the banquet, or the Red Death to the masquerade. Everybody knows that poets are idiotic and not politic. A poet will try to convince you that he, like George Blanda, represents the cause of serious child's play, and that Imagination can do the work of the Will.

This poet won't try to convince you that he belongs at this conference, except by invitation and out of curiosity. The last time he went to a crafts fair (in Winston-Salem) he saw little but masses of slipshod pots and objects that Sears, Roebuck and Company would hesitate to belabor us with. The last time he went to an exhibition of crafts, he was depressed by the "museumization" (Hilton Kramer's word) of what he saw—too much space, too much price, too much preciosity, things too freighted and too big. Once upon a time, objects had agoraphobia and stayed in homes, passing from one set of hands to another; and makers thought about sacramental relationships, authenticity, the numinous, and even William Morris's moral strictures—not about merchandise marts, filling up culture palaces and bank lobbies, and making the pages of *House Beautiful* and *House and Garden,* who declared loudly that now you can decorate with crafts at last and Marge and Bob Cretin down the block won't think you're tacky.

**180**

On a Pennsylvania dresser in my workroom in Highlands, North Carolina, I have six pots and vases: a Ch'ien Lung mirror-black; a tall Ming celadon; an alchemical form by M. C. Richards; a small, spotted Bernard Leach celadon; a plump, white piece by Toshiko Takaezu; and a polished black piece from the Santa Clara pueblo with eagle-feather design by Camillo Tafoya; on a wall behind them is a portrait of Charles Edward Ives, by W. Eugene Smith. A small quotation from the Shakers is pinned next to it: "No vice is with us the less ridiculous for being in fashion."

Why these ceramics, looming in the poet's scriptorium, when the poet couldn't make a pot to hiss in if his life depended on it? Charles Olson tells us:

> one loves only form,
> and form only comes
> into existence when
> the thing is born.

This will explain perhaps why I own ten versions of the Rachmaninoff *Third Piano Concerto* and never tire of comparing passages; and why I have added Jimmy Rowles, Ran Blake, John Lewis, Dave "Fingers" McKenna, and Fats Waller to my current shortlist of prime exemplars of the Universal Eighty-Eight; and why I take such joy in the fact of knowing that Anton Bruckner did not have his head into jogging. Who? What?

Gerry Williams suggested that "The Poetry of Work" should be the title of my paper. How can I be sure what he meant? ("The simplest words, we do not know what they mean unless we love and aspire," Emerson said.) There is no use expecting lucidity from J. Williams, Poet, derived from the Universe of Discourse or from the Cognitive Process; but, maybe, I can build a bit of a fire, using gists learned from poetry as kindling. Let there be light-wood!

The epitaph I wrote for Uncle Iv Owens, who farmed years ago up the highway toward Middle Creek Falls, runs as follows:

```
he done
what he could
when he got round
to it
```

which is as close as I can come to the elusive combination of Calvinist pessimism and the laconic wit you find in the Celtic people of the Southern Appalachians.

And this, setting down words of Aunt Creasy Jenkins, a formidable lady who lived her days in Highlands, North Carolina. She worked very hard, taking in wash from the summer people:

```
shucks
I make the livin

uncle
just makes the livin
worthwhile
```

Or this, from one of the ladies over near Penland School, in Mitchell County:

```
I figured
anything anybody
could do a lot of I
could do a little
of
mebby
```

One May, I heard a farmer near a place called Mouth of Wilson, Virginia, insist quietly that "the time to plant corn is when the seeds on the oak tree are the size of a squirrel's ear." I heard a farmer at Roaring Gap, North Carolina, says, "a good time to plant corn is when the hickory buds are big as a squirrel's foot." This is the minute, particular poetry of work—something to occupy the mind when it's not sweating. If you are

**182**

as busy as a jaybird's ass in mulberry season, you want the words to be *savory.*

Ever since Paul Goodman published an essay in *Dissent* (1958) called "Reflections On Literature As a Minor Art," poets and other writers with nothing to sell the deaf-ear society have been meditating gloomily on his conclusions: "In many ways literature has, in this century, become a minor art, more important than pottery or weaving, perhaps less important than block-printing or other graphics," and ". . . when we are called upon to teach our English and our Literature, we find ourselves like curators in a museum; the average student (like the average editor and publisher) no longer reads English like a native."

Even more repressive, if you happen to live in the Southland as I do about half the year, is the social order. The world is divided into the Nice People and the Just Plain Common. There are, of course, a few rich folks, busy as ever huntin' and fishin'. The black folks have been put out to separate-but-unequal pasture yet again. (I scarcely see a black person in the South anymore, unless he's an entertainer, a ballplayer, or a musician.) Ergo: no readers. The Nice People somehow know I agree with Gogol—that they are the *nasty* people—so they get the treatment in the tradition of Martial, H. L. Mencken, W. C. Fields, Jonathan Winters, B. Kliban, and me. The others simply have no inkling of the tradition, which makes the writer's desk a lonely place to be—easy to end up a dummy or a snob. I have a broadside on the wall over my desk: "By god, Jonathan, you know everybody, and that is why you are in trouble always. If you wish to compose a truthful poem, you will have to acquire a fine and solid sodality of enemies . . . Involuntarily, I live like an eremite. To whom can I talk besides a wise book? Have no doubt about it, I enjoy chattering as much as the next fool, but when I wish to ascend the Cordilleras, who is there to accompany me? Each man must go alone to his writings, to his adages, and to his grave." Edward Dahlberg wrote that to me in 1964.

Basil Bunting, aged 78, is perhaps the most distinguished poet living in England today. (If the Muse amounted to a hill of beans, you would know this.) It is dangerous, hopeless, and suspicious to try to define poetry. I might try to say it is a branch of manners, that it is a kind of music for the eye and for the ear, made out of words. *To record and elate*—for me those would be its primary functions. Poetry is traditionally a craft hard to come by, but particularly in a culture that does not value experience and age. "*Craft is perfected attention,*" as Ezra Pound one rephrased a Chinese notion.

I went to school with a series of hard taskmasters: Charles Olson, Louis Zukofsky, Kenneth Rexroth, Edward Dahlberg. They knocked sixty-five percent of the dross out of my poems and showed me how to condense. I went to men who knew how to do the job. I did not go to the university, where poetry is yet another subject matter to argue out as dialectic, with students feeling themselves the equal of the teachers, with everything "credited," putting the teachers in a better position for job-bargaining, eventual tenure, and so forth.

Now, at my age, I do not bother the venerable Zukofsky, but I still measure my work as a musical director of the *Macon County, North Carolina, Meshugga Sound Society* against the best I know: Catullus, Basho, and a dozen others; and, having failed to find much of a community of letters in the Republic (except in my own head, across time and space), I lean more and more to the non-literate, homemade world of the eccentric, the sorehead, the weird, the caitiff—particularly in the South. I have just spent a week in Georgia, documenting Miss Laura Pope's Museum in Pelham; palavering with St. EOM, the ineffable Eddie Owens Martin, who is building his temples and dancefloors that are sacred to Mu, Atlantis, shamans of the Creeks and Seminoles, Walt Whitman, and all that boogies all night; visiting the Reverend Howard Finster's version of the Garden of Eden, in Pennville. In May, I'll be in Kentucky, and I'll certainly want to drive up to Campton and see what Ed Tolson's been making over the winter. The words lie about him, ready to be fitted into poems with no trouble at all:

**184**

### STANDING BY HIS TRAILER-STUDIO
### IN CAMPTON, KENTUCKY, EDGAR TOLSON
### WHITTLES A FEW SYLLABLES

that piece
thats what some people call a *spinach*

i got it
offn a match box

it needs wings
and a lions tail

some damn woman down in Lexington
wants it

Lest I leave you fidgeting up in Campton with Ol' Ed: my most serious
poem lately, about vocation, takes place at Brigflatts Meeting House,
near Sedbergh, Cumbria. Since George Fox founded it in 1675, the Meet-
ing House has been a place of quiet worship:

### MY QUAKER-ATHEIST FRIEND, WHO HAS COME
### TO THIS MEETING HOUSE SINCE 1913, SMOKES &
### LOOKS OUT OVER THE RAWTHEY RIVER TO HOLME FELL

what do you do
anything for?

you do it
for what the medievals would call
something like
the *Glory of God*

doing it for money
that doesn't do it;

doing it for vanity,
that doesn't do it;

doing it to justify a disorderly life,
that doesn't do it

look at Briggflatts here . . .

it represents the best
that the people were able to do

they didn't do it for gain;
in fact, they must have
taken a loss

whether it is a stone next to a stone
or a word next to a word,
it is the *glory*—
the simple craft of it

and money, and sex aren't worth
bugger-all, not
bugger-all

solid, common, *vulgar* words

the ones you can touch,
the ones that yield

and a respect for the music . . .

what else can you tell 'em?

*(From* Apprenticeship In Craft,
*ed. by Gerry Williams.*
*Daniel Clark Books. Goffstown, NH, 1981)*

# "WHO KNOWS THE FATE
# OF HIS BONES?"

Sir Thomas Browne asked this question in 1658 in his book, *Hydrio-taphia, Urne-Buriall; or, a discourse of the sepulchrall urnes lately found in Norfolk.* A 20th century skeptic might reply to the English master of pomp and imagery: "Why do you want to know? I'm finding whatever the answer is not worth the asking."

I also love to visit cemeteries, which I don't consider *strange* at all. Connoisseurs of places and things necropolitan will all have their favorites: Woodlawn (the Bronx); Greenwood (Brooklyn); Mount Auburn (Cambridge); Forest Hills (Boston); Grove Street (New Haven); the Old Congressional Cemetery (Washington, DC); Forest Lawn (Hollywood); the burial grounds of Girod Street, St. Roch and St. Louis (New Orleans); and, perhaps best of all, Magnolia Umbra (outside Charleston). Some of the finest American sculpture of the 17th, 18th & 19th centuries is to be found in these calm, secretive sanctuaries.

Paris is full of treasures in Père Lachaise, Montparnasse, Passy and many others. London has Highgate and Nunhead. You can't begin to count everything in Italy, but the short list has to start off with: the Cimitero Monumentale in Milan; the vast Cimitero di Staglieno in Genoa; and the Catacombes of the Convento dei Cappuccini in Palermo. There is no avoiding the Cementerio de Las Corts in Barcelona, or Proton Nekrotaphion in Athens. These are just a few of the great cosmopolitan sites. I have missed many others simply because I wanted to find a revered artist on his own in proper isolation: Delius in Limpsfield; Samuel Palmer in Reigate; Frank Bridge on the South Downs of East Sussex; Stanley Spencer at Cookham; Walter Sickert at Bathampton . . . I am yet to pay my respects to Maurice Ravel, Jean Sibelius, John Sell Cotman, Paul Cézanne, Arnold Schoenberg, Carl Nielsen, Pierre Bonnard, and about a hundred others. (The only book I have seen that deals imaginatively with the European scene and offers anything even approaching the scope of *Scoring in Heaven* is Michael Ruetz's collection of photographs, *Nekropolis*, published by Carl Hanser in Munich, 1978.)

Lucinda Bunnen and Ginny Smith chose to visit *none* of the places above. Instead they spent seven months of 1980 travelling 26,000 miles to 677 cemeteries in places with names like: Paris (Tennessee), Monk's Corner, Electra, Runge, La Costa, Hohenwald, Nuba, Quartzsite, Terlingua, Labadieville, Point a la Hatch, Seguin, Zapata, Quihi, Socorro, Henryetta, Chickasha, Anadarka, Okemah, Pinos Altos, San Elizario, Goliad, Resaca, Acomita, Harmony Hill, Skull Valley, and Tombstone. Why? I just have to guess why two middle-class women from the dogwood-shrouded suburbs of Atlanta did this extraordinary thing.

They chose 1980, the beginning of a particularly mindless, predatory, politically vacuous decade in American life. The Times of Bonzo-Ronnie and George Butch were upon us—Sadie, bar the door! Times of junk-food, junk-bonds, junk-people, junk-emotions. The Predators, dressed by Brooks Brothers and J. Press, went to DC and declared war on sensuality, creativity, the ecology, and kindness. Back about the same time, a man of mixed-blood from Columbia, Missouri was also to make a journey into America. His name was Least Heat-Moon. He also called himself Bill Trogdon, after a grandfather eight generations back, William Trogdon, an immigrant Lancashireman, a miller on a piedmont river in North Carolina. His book, *Blue Highways*, seems to me as telling and interesting as William Bartram or Alexis de Tocqueville in earlier centuries. Least Heat-Moon got in his truck, "Ghost Dancing," and drove the little back roads to places nobody else had bothered to visit: ".... with a nearly desperate sense of isolation and a growing suspicion that I lived in an alien land, I took to the open in search of places where change did not mean ruin and where time and deeds connected." Another sentence: "Something always comes along and changes things. Mr. Down gets you every time."

When I first looked through several thousand slides and several hundred prints spread over the refectory table here at Skywinding Farm, I asked: "Lucinda and Ginny, don't you think *Scoring in Heaven* is too strange even to be a Jargon Society book?" They thought that was the nicest question anyone had ever asked them. I was, of course, just kidding. I love to visit The Strange like some people love to visit The Country, as I say over and over again. The Jargon Society has, after all, been the publisher of Ernie Mickler's glorious amalgam of pig-grease and sass, *White Trash Cooking*. And of Tom Patterson's monument to the late, bodacious Eddie Owens Martin of Buena Vista, Georgia, *St EOM in the Land of Pasaquan*. And we have espoused artists and poets as curious, visionary, "ugly," and far-off-the-interstates as Bill Anthony, Glen Baxter, Ralph Eugene Meatyard, Lyle Bongé, Doris Ulmann, Alfred Starr Hamilton, Mason Jordan Mason, and Richard Emil Braun. Stephen King says somewhere: "I guess when you turn off the main road, you have to be prepared to see some funny houses."

Perhaps one main lesson the eighties taught was that the Finer Things of Life were not so fine after all; and, another thing, that Nice People were anything but. Good reason to open the car door and disappear into the dark core of the democracy, where everything was as dumb as a two-dollar dog, where the folks were as good as the people, where you might just find a bit of human awe, ease, and connection with Eddie I. Johnson (Sept. 1933—Nov. 29, 1964), whose mother in McDonald, Tennessee had SCORING IN HEAVEN carved on his stone. Or, with John Richard Little (April 26, 1939—Nov. 26, 1976), who bowled a perfect game and found peace in a churchyard choking with kudzu near Fulton, Mississippi.

Item: there is a photograph of a man smiling and holding up a very considerable fish. It was taken in Harlan, Kentucky—a surprise in itself. (Them boys in Harlan are mean, you can't imagine that a Roman Catholic would live long enough to be buried there.) And this kind of enamelled medallion is exactly what one sees in *necropoli* from Spain to Greece. Here, are we not at the Pearly Gates themselves? Is the sportsman not smiling at the Big Fisherman Himself, saying: "Hey, Pete, baby, surely this large-mouthed bass is more than enough to get me in like flynn? I mean, when you add it to all those triple-frequent-flyer points—wow!"

Item: Tarpon Springs, Florida, three words on a granite cross: **INBI**, **MATHEMATICAL**, and **PRECISION**. Obviously not the familiar classical acronym for **JESUS OF NAZARETH, KING OF THE JEWS: INRI**. So is it: **INTERNATIONAL NOUGAT BITERS INC.**; or, **IRRATIONAL NUBIAN BANJO INSTRUMENTALISTS**; or, **ISLAMIC NEO BINOMIAL INTEGERS**??? The mind boggles, the bind moggles.

Item: a teddy bear wrapped in plastic ferns in Durham, NC, presiding over the fresh cake put out every year on the anniversary of the child's birth. Not like the food of the Egyptian mummy for its voyage to the Land of the Dead. Just something for the ants and chipmunks to eat.

Item: what are we to make of a six-foot Bugs Bunny in Styrofoam in Central City, Kentucky, flowers in one hand and an Easter basket full of carrots in the other? This time, maybe the mythic rabbit is truly a familiar for the child, a companion on the Road to Paradise. What about the grave of **TENNESEE WILLIUMS** in White Oak, New Mexico? Is the playwright's grave in St. Louis merely that of some worldly imposter? And then, there's the six-foot, green, cement Easter basket (with yellow handle) in Las Vegas, New Mexico, surrounded by a chain fence. Is that to protect it from the fierce Penitentes of the vicinity? Who was this man whose stone says only **SMITH**? How alone these monuments in remote houses of the dead seem. How tasteless. How imaginative.

Every time any of us gets in a vehicle (Least Heat-Moon's "Ghost Dancing," or Lucinda and Ginny's VW camper, "The Burro," or my Rabbit called "Okra"), we are trying, *desperately*, to refute a mordant observation by Edward Dahlberg, another lost nomad on our sere continent: "The only reason we travel is because there's no place to go." Ah, Edward, self-styled "Flea of Sodom," you might have hopped less and felt more at home away from the Cities of the Plain, if you had gone to find the granite stone of Edgar Tolson (1904–1984), "The Woodcarver." Very hard to find, on a little knoll above Hiram's Creek in the hills of eastern Kentucky, a couple of miles from the town of Campton, Wolfe County, a landscape destroyed by stripmining and clearcutting. There under the trees, the granite headstone of this remarkable artist, with a bronze cast of his self-portrait once whittled out of pine. How touching it is. So far, the vandals have left it all alone. And thus, there are the markers of the Outsiders to find in no cemetery at all. Another quest.

When Least Heat-Moon followed the blue highways into Tennessee, he managed to find: Only, Fly, Spot, Defeated, Pea Vine, Dull, Love Joy, Shake Rag, Peeled Chestnut, Clouds, Topsy, Ducktown, Wartburg, Miser Station, Weakly, Chuckey, and the sublimely named Nameless.

I can't believe he missed places I have circled from my journeys in Tennessee: Difficult, Curve, Vildo, Glimp, Owl City, Walnut Log, Hornbeak, Bells, Gates, Nutbush, Nankipoo, Gilt Edge, India, Skullbone, Brazil, Flowers, Sugar Tree, Skinem, Wheel, Bugscuffle, Bell Buckle, Love Lady, Hanging Limb, Sunbright, Royal Blues, Finger, and Soddy-Daisy? If our Atlanta photographers failed to probe these celestial spots, it's time they got back in "The Burro"!

Another thing: America being the great vacant, riotous, pullulating mess that it is, there is more to the blues and blue highways than grave markers. Right there in Glade Spring, Virginia (visited by Lucinda and Ginny) is the garden of the late Banner Blevins, complete with a concrete haint called "Dagger Woman" and a concrete "Preanderthal Man." Worth a visit. And, even more to the point, Glade Spring is where the extraordinary maker of clay pots, Georgia Blizzard, lives. William Blake would have enjoyed an afternoon with this spiritual woman and her "vessels," and so, I am sure, you, or Lucinda, or Ginny would. The pure people in America are so damn hard to find. When I first asked in the local hardware store in Glade Spring if an artist named Georgia Blizzard lived in the neighborhood, the sallow, middle-aged woman behind the counter said: "Well, there is somebody named Georgia Blizzard out Blue Hills Road, but she can't be no artist, she ain't got good clothes." Snobbery—you get it from the top, you get it from the bottom, because nobody cares very much, nobody has any time, and everything goes.

What to say and think about the images of *Scoring in Heaven*, we leave entirely up to you. The images are here in wonderful profusion. They are funny, sad, absolutely incredible, and made by photographers with good eyes and hearts. The one that (literally) haunts me is the one of the little violet spook, a playful little whangdoodle from a place called Carville, Louisiana. One more vapid speech by the incumbent in the White House, with his one facial expression; or, one more deception by his minions, Mr. Pisswater and Mr. Shatwater, and I may just have to get in the car and drive to Carville. After a visit to the cemetery, a man might just get himself a mess of mudbugs étouffée and hear a little zydeco. Moral: *get all the available good, and the bad will take care of itself.*

There's a superb interlude in *Blue Highways* between Least Heat-Moon and an old historian in Greenwich, New Jersey, on the Delaware Bay. Roberts Roemer says something that explains, by extrapolation, why *Scoring in Heaven* is important work. "The evidence of history, whether it's archives or architecture, is rare and worth preserving. It's relevant, it's useful. Here, it also happens to be beautiful. Maybe I've been influenced by the old Quakers who believed it was a moral question always to consider what you're leaving behind. Why not? It's not a bad measure of a man—what he leaves behind."

*(Introduction, rejected, to* Scoring in Heaven *by Lucinda Bunnen and Virginia Warren Smith, Aperture Publications, New York, 1991)*

# "BACK IN BLACK MOUNTAIN, A CHILE WILL SLAP YOUR FACE... BABIES CRYIN' FOR LICKER, AND ALL THE BIRDS SING BASS..." —BESSIE SMITH (WHO, ONE IMAGINES, NEVER MET ANNI AND JOSEF ALBERS)

lack Mountain College, North Carolina, United States of America..." must have sounded good to the ears of Anni and Josef Albers, at the Bauhaus, in the Nazi-infested quarter of Berlin-Steglitz in 1933. In Germany the name would be *Schwarzberg*, a name with a hint of the familiar *Schwarzwald* and so of that *Waldeinsamkeit* (forest solitude) that Germans revere in their souls, and that the Alberses must have yearned for in their own lives.

Black Mountain "just as well could be the Philippines," Anni Albers later recalled feeling when she finally stood on the steps of Robert E. Lee Hall, in the Blue Ridge Assembly Conference Center of the Protestant Episcopal Church, the first quarters of Black Mountain College, and looked out over the Swannanoa Gap to the Black Mountains, the highest range in eastern America. Black Mountain College might have fared better in the Philippines, come to think of it. 1933: in Buncombe County, where it was, there was Prohibition, and politicians like "Buncombe Bob" Reynolds were real-life equivalents of fictional stereotypes like Senator Claghorn, of radio fame. The novelist Peggy Bennett Cole, an early student of the Alberses', has noted that coming across them in "hillbilly setting, in the Southern Baptist Convention country of the Tarheel State, was a little like finding the remains of an advanced civilization in the midst of jungle."

In nearby Asheville, Kenneth Noland was nine years old. Also in Asheville, Tom Clayton Wolfe was piling up manuscripts for New York editors named Maxwell Perkins and Edward Aswell to package into "novels" and "prose poetry" for an audience that had read little but five poems by Keats and Joyce Kilmer, a bit of prose by Jean Stratton Porter, and Hervey Allen's *Anthony Adverse.* In Black Mountain town, Roberta Flack wouldn't be born for seven more years.

I first heard of the Alberses right here in Highlands, North Carolina, in 1947, from Clark and Mairi Foreman, delightful Southern renegades who liked cubist art and integrationalist politics. I saw a piece or two of Anni Albers' weaving. I got to Black Mountain College in 1951, two years after the Alberses had decamped, ultimately for Yale University. I caught a glimpse of Anni Albers at a superb lecture I heard her husband give in New Haven in 1958. She is 87, still there. I am still here.

Looking back into books about the Bauhaus and Black Mountain College, you find glimpses of Anni Albers and her husband that strike home. Once she wrote, "Very few of us can own things without being corrupted by them, without having pride involved in possessing them, gaining thereby a false security. Very few of us can resist being distracted by things. We need to learn to choose the simple and lasting instead of the new and individual. . . . This means reducing instead of adding, the reversal of our habitual thinking." (This is not the American wisdom of the Miss Piggy diet: "Don't eat anything you can't lift.") And Josef Albers counseled his students, "Please keep away from the bandwagon, from what is fashion and seems now successful or profitable. Stick to your own bones, speak with your own voice, and sit on your own behind."

"We be modesty persons," said Aunt Cumi Woody at Penland School once upon a time. Her quilts are cherished. I will forego Albers' high-culture student Bob Rauschenberg and keep my crafted attention on isolated poets (Lorine Niedecker, Alfred Starr Hamilton, Basil Bunting,

**194**

Mason Jordon Mason, Spike Hawkins) and country folks, artists and visionaries, like Henry Darger, Marion Campbell, Annie Hooper, Georgia Blizzard, and James Harold Jennings. James Harold lives out of Tobaccoville, NC and makes "thangs" out of wood. I have a piece called "Injun, Two Flowers, and Moon." James Harold says "Boys, it's all about the sun and the moon and the stars . . . and all them aeons. They'll keep you from gettin' nervous, they ain't got no death in 'em." Right now he's making a series of "Amazons," pronounced *A-may-zans*—with "real big garbonzas," as the distinguished drive-in movie critic Joe Bob Briggs might have written in his bizarre column for the Dallas *Times Herald*. James Harold doesn't even like to put a price on what he makes. He's a lonely man in a vacant place. He just likes to be sure people will come to see him and enjoy themselves. O Art World, take note.

*(From* Art Forum, *New York, April 1987)*

# THE TALISMAN

## BY STEPHEN KING & PETER STRAUB

ollectors please note that the first edition of *The Talisman* consisted of over 600,000 copies! The authors are perhaps as nervous about this fact as the reviewer is that his latest book of prose was limited to 5000 copies, and still it got remaindered.

H. L. Mencken says a nice thing: "When things get too unpleasant, I burn the day's newspaper, pull down the curtains, get out the jugs, and put in a civilized evening." I am a devoted fan of both Mr. King and Mr. Straub, and I love it that they so regularly provide me with a large book to read through the night. Robert B. Parker, another popular provider, gives us a new *Spenser* novel every year. Readers of Agatha Christie had this annual pleasure over the decades.

Can these guys write? Of course they can. I have read Stephen King's *The Shining* twice and, each time, had to stay up all night and race to the end—about noon the next day. The other one of Stephen King's that grabs me is *Salem's Lot*, his New England vampire job. Again: two readings haven't worn it out in my imagination. He said on television recently: "I don't worry about the critics. I am doing the best I can with what I've got." You take what you can get from writers, from friends, and from baseball players. One endured Harmon Killebrew at third or first, fumbling about on his piano legs, in order to see him come to the plate and lose one in the stands approximately every 14 1/2 times at bat. Mr. King can be as predictable and blue collar as McDonald's *bas-cuisine*, but, so what? He knows how to scare you, if that's what you want. And, every once in a while, he will remind you he was educated at the University of Maine and studied with such as Professor Carroll F. Terrell, the Poundian editor of *Paideuma* and *Sagetrieb*. A character will comment on the R. B. Kitaj prints in the dentist's office. Someone else will announce that he considers *For Love* to be Robert Creeley's best book of poems. You'll suddenly encounter a sentence that says, "Gee, I wish I was back in the frat house having arguments over the poetics of Charles Olson." Well, you won't get royalty checks amounting to much if you fuck around all your life over the poetics of Charles Olson. Never mind.

Peter Straub knows the prose of Mr. E. A. Poe, N. Hawthorne, H. James, and M. Twain. *Ghost Story* and *Floating Dragon* are eminently readable, but his major achievement to date is *If You Could See Me Now*, a spectral tale of the Midwest. I have consumed it start-to-finish *three* times and keep looking for the first editions of these two gentlemen, to add to my shelf next to such stylists as Robert E. Howard, Howard Phillips Lovecraft, and E. R. Eddison.

*The Talisman* is more adventure yarn than anything else—645 pages of it! The hero is a 12-year-old boy named Jack Sawyer, whose quest is to secure a talisman from a *black* hotel on the California coast in order to save his mother's life from cancer. To do this he is required to travel both the *real* America of hydrocarbons and fossil fuels, and a parallel world known as *the territories*. They exist side-by-side like stripes on a barger's pole. When the pole turns, the worlds blend. Jack Sawyer has the power to *migrate* or *flip* from one realm to the other. In *the territories* he is Jason, son of Queen Laura DeLoessian. Here, in New Hampshire, he is the son of Lily Cavanaugh, 'Queen of the Bs', 'Darling of the Drive-ins'. Jack is as good as his literary cousin, Tom Sawyer. He turns many heads.

"The kid! Jesus Christ! That kid!" exclaims a man named Buddy Parkins, shovelling chickenshit in a henhouse at dusk in a place called Goslin, Ohio. "He suddenly remembered the boy who had called himself Lewis Farren with the total clarity and a stunned kind of love. The boy who had claimed to be going to his aunt, Helen Vaughan, in the town of Buckeye Lane; the boy who had turned to Buddy when Buddy had asked him if he was running away and had, in that turning, revealed a face filled with honest goodness and an unexpected, amazing beauty—a beauty that had made Buddy think of rainbows glimpsed at the end of storms, and sunsets at the end of days that have groaned and sweated with work that has been well done and not scamped . . . He was suddenly overtaken by a sweet violent feeling of absolute adventure; never, since reading *Treasure Island*, at the age of twelve and cupping a girl's breast in his hand for the first time at fourteen, had he felt so staggered, so excited, so full of warm joy. He began to laugh. He dropped his shovel, and while the hens stared at him with stupid amazement, Buddy Perkins danced a shuffling jig in the chickenshit, laughing behind his mask and snapping his fingers."

Jack is yet another Stephen King avatar: a startling child with preternatural powers, threatened by the evil world of awake-and-asleep consciousness, and by fat tire salesmen on the road, slobbering to get into his underwear. The Puer Aeternus strikes again! Calling Ol' Doc Jung!

Well, the story goes on and on and on and it manages to take you along with it. There are memorable characters: Morgan Sloat, Speedy Parker, Wolf, Sunlight Gardener, and Jack's young cousin, Richie Sloat.

"So after many weeks, and hard adventuring, and darkness and despair; after friends found and friends lost again; after days of toil, and nights spent sleeping in damp haystacks; after facing the demons of dark places (not the least of which lived in the cleft of his own soul)—after all these things, it was in this wise that the Talisman came to Jack Sawyer . . ."

*(Unpublished, 1985)*

198

# HOMAGE TO ART SINSABAUGH
## (1924-1983)

## 1.

Arthur Reader Sinsabaugh was an irascible, wacko, Martini-gulping Dutchman—his forebear, Jan Vermeer, had equally crazy taste in red socks—, whose personal habits seemed to have little connection with his austere and superbly composed images of the landscape world. Consider another Dutchman, Piet Mondrian, the cigarette ashes dribbling all over the floor of his Broadway studio and two ears full of boogie-woogie—how do you figure what came out on the canvas? Art is hard enough without hanging 'Life' on its shoulder, like some new kind of Original Sin. Forget the rages and the stress. Behind his cameras, Art Sinsabaugh was a lovely and memorable guy, absolutely *passionate* about photography.

I knew him, now and again, over 32 years. We met one evening in the spring of 1951 at Hugo Weber's studio on North Avenue, Chicago. I was nicely loaded with J. W. Dant's bourbon (a raw and somewhat bellicose brand) and was ranting on about the collective deficiencies of the faculty of the Institute of Design to a select number of these worthies, lined up waiting to take abuse. A. R. Sinsabaugh, next in line, got redder and redder and was about to slug this haughty, southern, freshman apostate, when J. Williams had the wisdom to leave the room, throw up, and pass out on a bed covered with coats.

The next time we met was a decade later. After a poetry reading in Greeley, Colorado, I was heading for Champaign-Urbana to hear the premiere of Harry Partch's "Revelation in the Courthouse Park," April 11, 1961. Musicians from all over the country were en route to Illinois that weekend: Gil Evans, George Russell, and Peter Yates, to name three. I barely made it, halted by a freak blizzard in totally Funk, Nebraska, from where I dispatched amused postcards to the likes of Charles Mingus and John Handy. After the bodaciousness of the Partch, Alvin Doyle Moore (the Jan Tschichold of Taloga, Oklahoma) took me over to visit Sinsabaugh, who had let it be known that he no longer considered it a necessity to punch me into the ground in defense of academic credulity on the Near Northside of Chicago.

What I had in my briefcase was a little volume of Sherwood Anderson's *Mid-American Chants*. Kenneth Rexroth thought some of them deserved re-printing. So did Edward Dahlberg, who was ready to write an introduction. Seeing the work Sinsabaugh had been doing on the Illinois and Indiana landscapes with his banquet camera gave the key to the format and the content of the book. Between ourselves and the excellent design and printing afforded by *Low's Incorporated, Printers of Chicago* (Hayward R. Blake in charge of production), Jargon #45 was quite a book: 1550 copies @ $6.50 each.

*6 Mid-American Chants by Sherwood Anderson/11 Midwest Photographs by Art Sinsabaugh* is now a famous out-of-print book, fetching $400.00 a copy from the salivating dealers of New York and California. Twenty years ago this was, of course, hardly the case. One hundred and ninety-one copies were given out with compliments or for review. (I may be wrong, but I don't recall a single printed notice.) In the first six months we sold 247 copies. One hundred of these were bought by Henry Holmes Smith of Indiana University . . . Ten were ordered for Christmas presents by a Chicago businessman, who announced: "Hey, this looks like a class item!" ... The manager of the university bookstore in Champaign-Urbana refused to stock even one copy, saying: "You know how it is with these local poets." Some individual responses are interesting to record:

Otto Kerner, Governor, State of Illinois: "I particularly appreciate the Sherwood Anderson photos you so kindly sent . . ."

Charles Olson, poet, Gloucester, Massachusetts: "My God, it's like a train, like getting a train for Christmas, even including the tracks . . ."

Lorine Niedecker, poet, Fort Atkinson, Wisconsin: "The Sherwood Anderson rcd—its size, its horizontal depth absorb me like a mattress."

Ian Hamilton Finlay, poet, Edinburgh, Scotland: "The Longest Book in the World arrived safely inside its tarmacademed package (O groves of Tarmacademe!): was safely removed, a space cleared, and set down with only a few inches protruding through the specially opened lower window (swathed of course in tarpaulin). I no longer lack exercise: I just run up and down it, reading once a day. The photos are splendid, the production, conception, etc., beautiful."

Simpson Kalisher, photographer, New York City: "The Sinsabaugh/Anderson just came 10 minutes ago, I'm still smiling. It tickles me but I don't know why. My familiarity with life through a venetian blind is limited."

Harry Partch, composer, Van Nuys, California: "Unlike you, I do not have even 2 cubic feet I can call my own for storage, and I tend to resent a gift of anything that I will have to carry around with me the rest of my life—even as good as this . . ."

Paul Metcalf, writer, Chester, Massachusetts: "Yeah, sure, dad, it's great, but what do you do with the bloody thing? I don't have a Japanese teak table on which to make it Sacred Object of the Month." (Honorable publisher wrote humble author back, saying: "Suggest shoving honorable object up insolent Puritan fundament!")

And, last but not least, Edward Dahlberg, writer, Kansas City, Missouri, who was once insulted by Alfred Stieglitz Himself: ".... the Anderson book is utterly monstrous. Your emphasis on photography, a lazy stepmother art, is nonsensical. Both the *Mid-American Chants* and my "Note" are buried now beneath the snows of mere camera-work. So much money spent, and for what?—to put into the ground two doomed writers . . . 'Beware of a weak friend,' warned Pope, 'he is far more dangerous than a vehement and doughty foe . . .' "

The files also indicate that Mrs. William Carlos Williams ordered a copy for Charles Sheeler. And that Mrs. Sherwood Anderson, Ben Raeburn, James Laughlin, Sir Herbert Read, Grace Mayer, Helen Frankenthaler, and President Lyndon Johnson all strongly approved . . . And this final response. The book had been dedicated, in part, to the citizenry of the four prairie towns whose wisdom had preserved the original character of Louis Sullivan's banks; i.e., Owatonna, Minnesota; Columbus, Wisconsin; Grinnell, Iowa; and Sidney, Ohio. Mr. Clifford C. Sommer, President of the *Security Bank & Trust Company* of Owatonna, wrote, thanking me for a copy of the book and its inscription. He closed by saying:

> *Architectural Forum*, in its study of our remodeling work done in 1958, informally advised me that they made a broad search and believe that the restoration and preservation of the Security Bank Building in Owatonna is the only instance in the history of the country where business people spent time, effort, and money to preserve a major piece of architecture. There have been many committees and others who have done this, but they feel this was the first and only time a business, as such, has done it. We are indeed happy to be able to do this.

Sullivan takes me right back to the Sinsabaugh of those days. I remember his garden behind the house on the west side of Champaign. There was a border of Sullivan iron-work, undoubtedly preserved for Art by the late Richard Nickel. Sullivan with corn and native grasses—just right under the Champaign County sunshine . . . And that pops a few more images into place: Sinsabaugh, in his foreign-correspondent-type London raincoat, in a local dive, squeezing the volatile oils out of a twist of lemon, setting it afire on the surface of a Martini (straight up)—his special recipe . . . Sinsabaugh, in battered blue station-wagon, one sporting red flags and sirens and flashing lights to get him though urban traffic more quickly when he demanded it . . . Sinsabaugh, suddenly throwing out both arms and doing a violent twist to the left and to the right—something to do with tension in his back. His timing tended to be quite dramatic in such instances, suggesting Lennie Bernstein engulfed in the big climax in the first movement of Mahler's *Second.*

The last time together was the summer of 1979, when Tom Meyer and I invited Sinsabaugh to visit us in Dentdale, Cumbria in the northwest of England, and to bring the banquet camera. That country of Pennine Fells had yet to find a great landscape photographer to record its unique qualities. It still hasn't. Art had a difficult three months, couldn't cope physically with the camera equipment (the reasons for this are explained further along in this piece), and just *couldn't,* generally, see eye to eye with the demands of a couple of poets. Despite no silver prints at all, a Sinsabaugh activity report made to his university department claims the existence of four hundred 35-mm color slides. These I have not seen—has anyone? One hopes they are part of the Sinsabaugh Archive at Indiana University in Bloomington.

## 2.

It was not difficult to get Art Sinsabaugh talking volubly and enthusiastically about the work of Harry Callahan or Aaron Siskind or Henry Holmes Smith or Minor White or Frederick Sommer or even Clarence John Laughlin. He was generally quiet about himself. But here are a few of the more telling instances:

> I drove and I drove and I drove and I drove. It must have taken an hour and
> a half and as I passed the last hot-dog stand, I realized I was in the country,

but so much so, so much in the country, that there just wasn't anything there, nothing . . . I was looking for what I knew and did not *see* that which I did not know . . . At some point I became aware of the unbelievable infinite detail on the horizon; this is what drew my attention. So I set about to pursue the distant horizon. I cut the foreground off and part of the sky to accentuate this horizon-line activity. But the more I looked at them, the more I realized they weren't as full as expression of this great vastness of the prairie as I had wished to portray. I wasn't aware that I was seeking a peripheral kind of quality in the photographs. I knew that my response to the prairie forced me to turn my head left and right. I would be kind of all taken in by the tremendous sweep before me . . . When I accidentally came across the old Corona 12″ × 20″ banquet camera, I immediately decided this was the camera for me.

■

Have the calotype process, the daguerreotype, the tintype, the ambrotype, the collodion process, the panoramic camera been fully explored? Could not these processes and others, if properly used, lead us further insights into a more vital visual experience? . . . I appeal then for a critical re-evaluation of the discarded techniques of photography to enhance the images of the future.

■

It is my intention to continue to express my feelings about the rural and urban landscape of America through photography . . . I also want to photograph in other regions of the country, to distill the essence of the mountains of New England, the shores of the Eastern Seaboard, and the marshes of the South . . . I do not want to force the long, narrow horizontal format on each area but rather I want to let the subject matter dictate how it must be handled . . . There is yet much to be done and I am anxious to start.

■

I suppose everyone looks forward to a sabbatical. Some perhaps even live for a sabbatical. Since I died twice in the physical sense, during the Spring 1976 semester, I feel that this sabbatical was a celebration of my rebirth . . .

**204**

Since my work of photography causes me to see what is not always obvious to others, I had a renewed pleasure in really seeing with a new insight. All that I had seen before took an entirely different meaning; that which I had always loved I still loved; that which I had not admired but had really detested I no longer felt bitter about. I had no need to ridicule this badly through photography. I could only see it, ignore it, and drive on. For one who has had a great deal of difficulty in ignoring *anything* that has touched me in my lifetime, this was a new and I think a great surprise.

■

. . . Harper & Row (N.Y.C.) wrote, expressing interest in publishing the *Chicago Landscape* work as a book. When I made a trip to New York to see them they said they would like to get an 'important person' like Nelson Algren to do the text. I said: "No thank you; I want my work to stand or fall on its own."

## 3.

I've just spent two days staring out over the New Mexico prairie in the direction of Portales, while reading texts by four enthusiasts of the Midwestern Landscape: Frank Lloyd Wright, John Root, Louis Sullivan, and Lewis Mumford. *Enthusiast*, a good word. It means one who is possessed by a god. Here, for Art Sinsabaugh, is a distillate of a few of their words––evidence of "intensity on the far horizon" . . .

> as anyone might see,
> a beech tree is a beech tree . . .

■

> a building
> dignified as a tree
> in the midst of
> nature

■

I see this extended horizontal line
as the true earth-line of human life,
indicative of freedom always.

The broad expanded plane
is the horizontal plane,
infinitely expanded.
In that lies such freedom
for man on this earth
as he may call his.

■

to think
is to deal in simples—
with an eye
single to the altogether

to know what to leave out and
what to put in;
just where and just how,
ah, *that*
is to have been educated
in knowledge of simplicity . . .

■

the joe-pie weed
and the swamp maple
and the locust tree
were extirpated
in favor of
a few elegant, sickly shrubs
which could not flourish
in the common soil
of our life

■

a song
in the green woods

his imagination has risen
to meet the expectation of the land

out of the ground; into the sun!

## 4.

ARTHUR READER SINSABAUGH: A.R.S., LATIN FOR *ART*.
*Ars longa, vita brevis est!*

*(Aperture 95, New York, 1984)*

# JCD

friend in Kentucky just sent me his translations of Antisthenes. Say *who?* I must assume him to be the stern brother of Antonomasia, yet another darling of the gods whose name rings but faintly in our ignorant, post-modern ears. Anyway, Antisthenes is said to have said: "Socrates told his students to know themselves. He couldn't guarantee that they had the equipment." I was brought up on such lovely, literate wickedness from the tongue of John C. Davis, the Squire of Nutley, New Jersey. Had he been a cracker-barrel sage from Bagdad, Kentucky, he might have invoked a more native aura and uttered: "You can't hit what you don't swing at!" In springtime in the Kentucky Blue-Grass, the male imagination fixes upon the mountain ash and the fine Louisville Slugger bats made from its limber wood.

For the young Jonathan C. Williams, it was John C. Davis who made all the difference. Academies (including rather good ones like St. Albans School) are designed to promote what is boring, self-perpetuating, Jewish/Christian, middle-class, and heterosexual. Some incorrigible bohemians like myself had other fish to fry. It was JCD's remarkable prescience to respect vast differences in his students—to introduce them to Frederick Delius and Fats Waller if money-in-the-bank formalists like J. S. Bach and L. von Beethoven did not ring the aesthetic gong. Not only did JCD's world have a range that inspired any but those too dumb to know how to pour piss out of a boot (even if the instructions were printed on the heel), but he also tried to teach charity (Christian, and beyond) and proper manners to his charges. He must be one of the great gentleman-teachers, *ever.*

I left St. Albans with genuine home-made equipment, refined and mostly unimpaired by routine. I received from JCD the rudiments of paying close attention, of looking and recording, of listening and keeping quiet when the moment demanded it. This is what allows grace in a writer. Not that JCD was alone in this epic work. That excellent, whimsical stork of an artist, Dean Stambaugh, would drag me down to the Phillips Gallery and make me burst with merriment in front of Redon or Ryder until, sobered up, I'd realize what these painters were celebrating: *human difference.* And Ferdinand Ruge, the seeming antithesis to the Davis/Stambaugh style, also devoted more energy than he should have to teach one to get the right words in the proper places. The *simple* craft—so *hard* to learn.

Teaching did not end in the classroom. One is always ripened by conversation with John Davis, in Washington, DC, or Highlands, North Carolina. I, for one, want much more of it. I wish him a future with a hearth and a desk and friends to sit with under the maples. And a fantastic cat (with a passion for Italian Opera that not even JCD could get me to like). A best beast on the order of Edward Lear's feline friend, "Old Foss."

(J. Williams, '47)

*(From* Some Commentaries on the Teaching Career of John Claiborne Davis at St. Albans School, *edited by Brice M. Clagett, '50, privately published, Washington, DC, June 1983)*

# VIRGINIA RANDALL WILCOX
## (1909-1991)

**W**hen Ted Wilcox died the other night up on Billy Cabin Mountain, Highlands lost a very notable citizen. I mourn the person, some-one I have known for 43 years, and my first responses to the news were these three. To remember some words by Butler Jenkins, who used to caretake for the Wilcoxes: "You live until you die—if the limb don't fall." . . . to remember some lines voiced by Ted, as Miss Harmony Blue-blossom, in William Saroyan's play *The Beautiful People*: "Things end. That's what makes them things." . . . and to remember what Miss Lucy Morgan, of Penland School, told me once about Aunt Cumi Woody, a re-vered mountain woman and maker of quilts: "She is gone . . . she enjoyed her days." Even a few weeks ago, with hardly any voice left and sadly confined to a wheelchair, Ted looked exactly like Queen Elizabeth the First of England, ready to read the riot act at one and all: "NO FOOL-ISHNESS! Get on with the business of leading your life."

George Bernard Shaw defined a lady or a gentleman as someone who treated everyone the same. I've known miles of snobs and people con-vinced they are better than you and me, but I have met few ladies and gentlemen. Ted was one of the first. And certainly one of the first South-ern women "of her class" who had managed to become an adult with a brain. A conversation with Ted did not go around Robin Hood's barn.

There was no mention of having to go to the little girl's room. She was a straight-talking, democratic idealist to the core. The Bible speaks of many having "feeble purpose and low ideal" and of "willful blindness to Thy presence and deafness to Thy call." There's no way that non-passionate shoe fit Ted Wilcox. She loved blessed people and she loved arguing with cussed people. Think of the people in the Highlands community she knew: Ralph Mowbray, Ralph & Louise Sargent, Overton Chambers, Mary Brown, Elizabeth Edwards, Fergus Kernan, "Scratch" Reese, Marjorie Gumble, Steve Potts, Aunt "Creasy" Jenkins, Maxie Wright, Arnold Keener, Doc Howell, Tom Krumpler, Chuck Wick, Bob Dupree, Lindsay & Jeannie Olive, Gertrude & Dolly Harbison, Henry Wright, John Burnett, Sara Gilder, Arthur & Sara Little, Fred Allen, Jim Hines, Tom & Beverly FitzPatrick, Manson Valentine—what a spectrum! I name a handful, she knew hundreds.

A lady with a sharp wit, sharpened no doubt from being married to Jack Wilcox, semi-pro ballplayer, professor of economics, one of God's Angry Men, a man who suffered fools not at all, who despised the Primitive Mind, as he called it, who lamented a world increasingly run by boobs, greedies, and bullies. It has been suggested that literature is the way we ripen ourselves by conversation. Then, surely, a lot of my literary education took place on the porch of Farmhouse, up on Billy Cabin Mountain, sipping bourbon, rocking in a rocking chair, talking about people named John Dewey, Alexander Meiklejohn, Gunnar Myrdal, John Andrew Rice, Stringfellow Barr, Robert M. Hutchins, and Lewis Mumford. One talked about diversity and the need for much more kindness in the society; about Jews and black people; about bigots and their victims of all kinds. One talked of Willie Mays and the Babe; of God, and the price of towelling.

How I'd like to sit before the fireplace at Farmhouse this snowy day and talk to Jack & Ted about "the latest." It seems that drugs, financial greed, poverty, and AIDS are not enough for our poor republic. Now, President George "Let's Kick Some Butt" Bush and Saddam Gomorrah have consigned us to the Fires of Islam for the special bargain price of only a billion bucks a day. I wonder what the Wilcoxes would say to a note I just received from a politically alert friend in London? He writes: "The facts that Saddam Hussein was set up in Iraq by the CIA and that Kuwait was indeed stolen from Iraq by the British 30 years ago, are, of course, completely suppressed over here." Little is beyond belief. But, maybe, as the communitarian she was, Ted would be able to offer even wiser counsel about a troubling local matter: how to best address the problems of our friend, Lawrence Wood? From what it says in *The Highlander*, he's ill and needs heat, water, and food. Ted would have read her Sherwood Anderson and recognized the fragility of a Lawrence Wood in his cast of country characters. I hope, even without Ted, Highlands can figure out how to take care of one of its own?

Well, the play is over, Miss Harmony Blueblossom. Time to feed the birds and put on the happiest music you know: the delectable variations on the song, "The Trout," in the Piano Quintet in A major, D. 667, by the young Franz Schubert.

*(from* The Highlander, *Highlands, NC, January 29, 1991)*

# "HIYA, KEN BABE, WHAT'S THE BAD WORD FOR TODAY?"

They've never made a movie about Kenneth Patchen (1911–1972). Now they're too late. The only guy who could play him, Robert Mitchum, has just died. He had the voice, the build, and the sleepy eyes. He had the laconic barroom style to deliver a poem like "The State of the Nation," whose last line I have altered in the title above.

It's difficult to fathom why he's not read by the young these days. Do the young have enough grounding to read any unconventional poet these days? Basil Bunting always insisted there were still plenty of "unabashed" boys and girls about, but their slovenly teachers had never trained them in the literature that mattered. There were three or four decades when Kenneth Patchen was a poet who mattered a lot to a lot of people. I was having lunch last autumn with J. Laughlin, Patchen's old friend and his publisher at New Directions. He shook his head, sadly, "they just don't read Kenneth anymore—how can we understand that?" I don't think we can understand. Each century produces a Blake and a Whitman, a Ryder and a Bruckner. They didn't arrive out of the empyrean with fan clubs and Web sites.

Patchen wrote at a time when most writers stayed home and wrote, in places like Rutherford, Old Lyme, Fort Atkinson, and Sausalito. The previous generation was into celebrity and reporters followed them to Pamplona, the rue de Fleurus, and Rapallo. Patchen had to stay home, and stay in bed—his wrecked back gave him no mercy. Except for a few sessions of poetry-and-jazz with Charles Mingus in New York in the late 1950s, and with the Chamber Jazz Sextet in California, Patchen was a private man, not on stage.

It is instructive, perhaps, to contrast this kind of life with that of two later poets who have recently died: Allen Ginsberg and James Dickey. Both of these men spent early years working in public relations on Madison Avenue and neither stopped jabbering for a single second thereafter. Ginsberg was a mensh. His desire to be the spokesman of his generation was the last thing I could imagine or would want, but we always enjoyed being together on what were rare occasions in San Francisco, New York, or here in Dentdale. He upset a lot of squares, he opened up liberating avenues, he put himself on the line; but, may I be excused if I have to say that most of the poetry struck me as hard-sell advertising. I was reminded more of Walter Winchell and Gabriel Heater and Paul Harvey than of the Buddha . . . Sheriff Dickey, more bubba than mensh, was unbelievably competitive. At a poetry occasion in the White House put on by Rosalynn Carter and Joan Mondale, Jim barely had time to shake my hand. He whispered to his wife, "Come on, honey, we got to go work the crowd." He never forgave me for writing to someone that *Deliverance* was about as accurate to goings-on in Rabun County, Georgia, as Rima the Bird-Girl was in *Green Mansions*, by W. H. Hudson. I also made the mistake of quoting Mr. Ginsberg on *Deliverance*: "What James Dickey doesn't realize is that being fucked in the ass isn't the worse thing that can happen to you in American life." Compared to these public operators, Patchen was as remote as one of the Desert Fathers. (The Desert Fathers are not a rock group.)

I sat in Concourse K at O'Hare Airport in Chicago recently, reading *The New York Times* and *Fanfare* and watching the Passing Parade for about three hours. This is very sobering work. I'm not sure I saw one individual who was dressed individually. Most people looked like mall-crawlers. Most people looked over-active and stressful. They were moving at speed, like the ants in a formicary. Others were merely bland and moved like wizened adolescents. It would be futile to suggest any sign of appetite amongst these citizens for Kenneth Patchen, or J. V. Cunningham, or Wallace Stevens or James Laughlin. A few people waiting for the evening flight to Manchester were reading paperbacks purchased at the airport. John Grisham and Danielle Steel and Dean Koontz were most in evidence. (One young man was reading Camus, but we must pretend he doesn't exist.) I decided to buy *The Door to December*, by Dean Koontz, "a number one *New York Times* bestselling author who currently has more than 100 million copies of his books in print."

> . . . Whatever the cause of his crumbling self-control, he was becoming undeniably more frantic by the moment.
>
> Wexlersh.
>
> Manuello.
>
> Why was he suddenly so frightened of them? He had never liked either of them, of course. They were originally vice officers, and word was that they had been among the most corrupt in that division, which was probably why Ross Mondale had arranged for them to transfer under his command in the East Valley; he wanted his right-hand men to be the type who would do what they were told, who wouldn't question any questionable orders, whose allegiance to him would be unshakable as long as he provided for them. Dan knew that they were Mondale's flunkies, opportunists with little or no respect for their work or for concepts like duty and public trust. But they were still cops . . .

That goes on for 510 pages. So, fellow-stylists, there is hope for us all, whether you like square hamburgers or round hamburgers. I go for the round ones, as I am sure Mr. Koontz does. McDonald's has sold over 90 billion of the little buggers. Here's to LitShit and a kilo of kudzu up the kazoo!

New York publishers calculate the fate of the American novel is in the hands of 5000 readers who will actually purchase new hardback fiction.

At the Jargon Society we would be delighted to sell 500 copies of the latest poetry by Simon Cutts or Thomas Meyer. It might take ten years. Of course, out there in the real world, thousands of verse-scribbling plonkers crank out a ceaseless barrage of what Donald Hall calls the McPoem. Oracles in high places proclaim a Renaissance of Poetry. A distributor tells me of the purchase of 20,000 hardback copies by a woman poet I have never read nor heard of. The hermits and caitiffs I hang out with don't explore other parts of the literary jungle and just stick to their Lorine Niedecker and Basil Bunting, and even drag out volumes of Kenneth Patchen when the fit is on them. We few, we (occasionally) happy few . . .

How did we odd readers find our way to Kenneth Patchen? He, of course, would never have been in the curriculum at St. Albans School or at Princeton, my adolescent stamping grounds. I stumbled across a pamphlet by Henry Miller, *Patchen: Man of Anger & Light*. Miller I knew about because evil *Time* magazine had so vilified his book, *The Air-Conditioned Nightmare*, that I took the next bus to Dupont Circle in Washington, DC, and bought it at the excellent bookshop run by Franz Bader. By the time I was ten I had the knack of discovering the books important to me beyond those required at school. But, I was lucky. I had three good teachers in prep school and I lived in a city with real bookstores. And reading books was something you did. Nowadays, books are a form of retro-delivery-system with no cord to plug in. Way uncool.

By the time I was twenty and dropped out of Princeton to study painting and printmaking and graphic design, I was into Patchen in a big way. I read him along with Whitman, Poe, H. P. Lovecraft, William Carlos Williams, e.e. cummings, Edith Sitwell, Robinson Jeffers, Hart Crane, Kenneth Rexroth, Thoreau, Randolph Bourne, Kropotkin, Emma Goldman, Henry Miller, and Paul Goodman. Before I was twenty-five I owned the manuscripts of *The Journal of Albion Moonlight* and *Sleepers Awake*. I had over forty of Patchen's painted books and a few watercolors. I'd published KP's *Fables & Other Little Tales* during my stay in the medical corps in Germany. What was the attraction?

**216**

Patchen was an original. Someone said, equally, of Babe Ruth: "It's like he came down from out of a tree." He was ready to play. Patchen and the Babe were heavy hitters, and nobody struck out more. There is a towering pile of Patchen poems that amounts to not much. But, he really does have 20 or 25 poems that seem as good as anybody's. He had power, humor, intuitive vision, and a kind of primitive nobility. He knew his Blake and Rilke. He loved George Lewis's clarinet and Bunk Johnson's cornet. He drew fabulous animals and painted very well. There was nobody like him.

A few examples. "The State of the Nation" is from *First Will & Testament* (1939):

> Understand that they were sitting just inside the door
> At a little table with two full beers and two empties.
> There were a few dozen people moving around, killing
> Time and getting tight because nothing meant anything
> Anymore
> Somebody looked at a girl and somebody said
>     Great things doing in Spain
> But she didn't even look up, not so much as half an eye.
> Then Jack picked up his beer and Nellie her beer
> And their legs ground together under the table.
> Somebody looked at the clock and somebody said
>     Great things doing in Russia
> A cop and two whores came in
> And he bought only two drinks
> Because one of them had syphilis
>
> No one knew just why it happened or whether
> It would happen again on this fretful earth
> But Jack picked up his beer and Nellie her beer again
> And, as though at signal, a little man hurried in,
> Crossed to the bar and said Hello Steve to the bartender.

Painting by Edward Hopper, piano by Hoagy Carmichael—very evocative stuff. The music in the poem is slow, bluesy, uncomplicated. Here's another I like in similar vein, "Lonesome Boy Blues," from *Orchards, Thrones & Caravans* (1952):

> Oh nobody's a long time
> Nowhere's a big pocket
> To put little
> Pieces of nice things that
> Have never really happened
> To anyone except
> Those people who were lucky enough
> Not to get born
>
> Oh lonesome's a bad place
> To get crowded into
> With only
> Yourself riding back and forth
> On
> A blind white horse
> Along an empty road meeting
> All your
> Pals face to face
>
> Oh nobody's a long long time

And then there is the Patchen of social injustice, who keeps asking "I wonder whatever became of human beings?" "The Orange Bears," from *Red Wine & Yellow Hair* (1949), sets you up and asks just what kind of punch you can take:

> The orange bears with soft friendly eyes
> Who played with me when I was ten,
> Christ, before I left home they'd had
> Their paws smashed in the rolls, their backs
> Seared by hot slag, their soft trusting

Bellies kicked in, their tongues ripped
Out, and I went down through the woods
To the smelly crick with Whitman
In the Haldeman-Julius edition,
And I just sat there worrying my thumbnail
Into the cover—What did he know about
Orange bears with their coats all stunk up with soft coal
And the National Guard coming over
From Wheeling to stand in front of the millgates
With drawn bayonets jeering at the strikers.

I remember you could put daisies
On the windowsill at night and in
The morning they'd be so covered with soot
You couldn't tell what they were anymore.

A hell of a fat chance my orange bears had!

Severity, gravity, and wistful sadness. Patchen worked this combination to great effect in *The Famous Boating Party* (1954). He tells the poem like a good shaggy-dog story and he knows how to time and place the punch line just right. Here are two prose-poems, "Soon It Will" and "In Order to":

### SOON IT WILL

Be showtime again. Somebody will paint beautiful faces all over the sky. Somebody will start bombarding us with really wonderful letters . . . letters full of truth, and gentleness, and humility . . . Soon (it says here) . . .

### IN ORDER TO

Apply for the position (I've fogotten now for what) I had to marry the Second Mayor's daughter by twelve noon. The order arrived at three minutes of.
    I already had a wife; the Second Mayor was childless: but I did it.
    Next they told me to shave off my father's beard. All right. No matter that

he'd been a eunuch, and had succumbed in early childhood: I did it, I shaved him.

Then they told me to burn a village; next, a fair-sized town; then, a city; a small down-at-heels country; then one of "the great powers;" then another (another, another)—In fact, they went right on until they'd told me to burn up every man-made thing on the face of the earth! And I did it, I burned away every last trace, I left nothing, nothing of any kind whatever.

Then they told me to blow it all to hell and gone! And I blew it all to hell and gone (oh, didn't I) . . .

Now, they said, put it back together again; put it all back the way it was when you started.

Well . . . it was my turn to tell *them* something! Shucks, I didn't want any job that bad.

I hope some of you reading this will connect with Kenneth Patchen—he's real good people. New Directions keeps quite a few paperbacks in print. My copy of the *Collected Poems* is inscribed from Kenneth to me, September, 1969:

> as we were, we are, my friend
>
> *If the Lord is willin'*
> *And the creeks don't rise*

(Conjunctions: 29, *Annandale-on-Hudson, 1997*)

# JAMES LAUGHLIN (1914-1997)

think we have a proper candidate, finally, for the excellent "Epitaph for Someone or Other," from J. V. Cunningham's little book, *Doctor Drink*. It goes:

> Naked I came, naked I leave the scene,
> And naked was my pastime in between.

At the end of his long literary life which spanned nearly 70 years, J. Laughlin left us a cache of poems that makes me ask an interesting question: did the classic Roman masters (Horace, Catullus, Martial, Propertius, Ovid), did they leave as many excellent poems amongst the whole lot of them as the Master of Meadow House just on his own? This is not a captious or whimsical question. It may take us a generation or two to come to an enlightened answer.

What I am suggesting is that Laughlin poems are available to us by the hundreds in their finely-crafted simplicity and clarity. We know the world they are about. To the reader without considerable Latin, poor Catullus is hard going and often you wonder why anyone bothers. A prose translation on the order of F. W. Cornish's published in the Loeb Classical Library in 1913 is by now utterly pallid, de-sexualized, and inanimate. Frank O. Copley gave us in the 1950s a raucous version seen through the prisms of e.e. cummings. A strange thing to do—sometimes charming. There is even an edition of 1970 for "American Readers" translated by Reney Myers and Robert J. Ormsby. It's down-market and chattery, full of chicks and pricks, and brings some of the briefer epigrams to life: "Pricko tries to climb the poets' hill; / The Muses with their pitchforks praise his skill." The modern version that gives us more feeling of Catullus's cultivation-cum-sass in the Rome of his day is the one by the late Peter Whigham that is published in Penguin Classics.

To change tack—JL, distinguished poet, distinguished publisher, was also an accomplished skier, to judge from reports by Kenneth Rexroth and Hayden Carruth. I am sure they are right, but I am writing as a man who spent two years in Aspen, Colorado in the 1960s and never once bothered to lift up mine eyes unto the hills to see anyone streaking down the slopes of Aspen Mountain. I was busy at the Aspen Institute, cogitating, and playing volleyball with strange people like Hunter Thompson, Jonas Salk, James Farmer, Barry Bingham, and George Plimpton's father . . . JL's pipes and cigars were other major pleasures he allowed us to know about. His golf game he kept private.

What is the *one* adjective that most described his manner of being? Rexroth said it was JL's "chaste" demeanor. He was not a man who caroused or drank much of anything. You certainly felt his Scots-Irish Presbyterian reservation. Being in the presence of an abstemious Celt is frankly unsettling, like observing a famous but cadaverous chef.

I think "dogged" is the word I would use. This quality allowed him to struggle through all those piles of hideous manuscripts looking for something, *anything* with quality. It kept him absolutely devoted to the hard process of writing his poems and prose over decades when few ever gave them more than a thought. And, of course, it kept him on erotic patrol from about the age of 13 to 83. Georges Simenon (who wrote 400 books, of which 300 were very good, according to Guy Davenport) insisted that he'd slept with over 12,000 women. His seemingly non-long-suffering wife would laugh loudly and insist it was a figure definitely less than 7,000. So, as they say, who's counting? Those high in testosterone and those low in testosterone probably don't think about sex more than three times a minute. That leaves plenty of time for novel-writing. It is, after all, a "low form," sayeth the poet, quoting some wag like Mr. Mencken.

J. Laughlin saw himself with startling clarity. There are not many poems around like "Reading the Obituary Page in *The Times*":

> He was a messy sort of person
> who never quite finished any-
>
> thing he started   there was a
> garden of girls who had found
>
> him unsatisfactory for one rea-
> son or another   with men friends
>
> he was the master of the short
> conversation   after ten minutes
>
> there was really nothing more to
> say   the truth was that he dis-
>
> liked himself extremely   he had
> to press his brains against his
>
> skull to understand anything
> more difficult than the news-
>
> paper   all his life he never
> understood what made a car
>
> run   computers were out
> of the question   in old age he
>
> became foolish about money try-
> ing to make more go out than

came in    this annoyed the bank
and worried the children he

didn't kill himself but he
constructed his death as if

he were drawing diagrams
for a newly born Euclid

Not exactly *luxe, calme, et volupte.* More like calm, cool, and collected. I made my visits to Meadow House, Norfolk, Connecticut, for some 35 years and certainly shall miss them in the extreme. True to his poem, some days the sands of conversation would start running out after ten minutes. Then, you had to figure out something to shift JL from his Squire Sisyphus mode into his more garrulous Hiram Handspring persona. All one had to do was whisper a name like "Edward Dahlberg" or "Merle Hoyleman" or "Kenneth Rexroth" and the fat would hit the fire. We would babble on happily for the 45 minutes until lunch and, with a bit of luck, I might even be able to sneak a second Scotch and soda from the sideboard in the dining room.

The living room/study at Meadow House is a marvelous room. The extraordinary shelves of private press books, éditions de luxe, artist's books; the glimpses here and there of Marin, Klee, Chirico, Tchelitchev, Magritte; the big desk covered with manuscripts and New Directions business; the large windows looking out over the rocky meadow and the sheep. Somewhere Ezra Pound says, "The humane man has amity with the hills." I have been in equally civilized parlors (Guy Davenport's, Robert Kelly's, Ping Ferry's, Peyton Houston's, Jonathan Greene's, Robert Duncan's, Donald Anderson's, to name a few), but nothing quite like this. Smoke damage to some of the paintings was severe in a fire a few years back. A late-night cigar fallen and smoldering in the cushion of JL's favorite Queen Anne armchair. Rare books too were lost, but, wondrously, not the house, nor anybody. Last year things looked much as always. I hope that room can remain itself. What a day out, to visit Meadow House and then drive an hour east to Mark Twain's superb domicile in Hartford.

At JL's death I heard Mr. Roger Straus on NPR's "Morning Edition" lament that Laughlin was the Last of the Gentleman Publishers and we would not see his like again. I think people in New York City should travel more. JL was not the first such publisher. There were Alfred Knopf, Kurt Woolf, Pascal Covici, Horace Liveright, John Farrar, just to start an eminent list. In 1997 two of JL's most talented contemporaries also died: Leslie Katz, of Eakins Press; and Ben Raeburn, of Horizon Press. There is a younger generation of publishers very much in the New Directions tradition. Think of Douglas Messerli at Sun & Moon Press; John Martin at Black Sparrow Press; Jonathan Greene at Gnomon Press; Tom Meyer and myself at the Jargon Society; The Press of David Godine; Lawrence Ferlinghetti at City Lights Books; and Jack Shoemaker at North Point and Counterpoint. There are obvious others. J. Laughlin was not the first or the last. Let us just say he was the BEST.

Small Coda:

### LINES WRITTEN DURING A PITTSBURGH STEELERS/ NEW ENGLAND PATRIOTS AFC PLAYOFF GAME*, IN HONOR OF THE MASTER OF MEADOW HOUSE

*Ave, Catulle!*

Your Frater Jacobus is nearing the Elysian Fields. Bid him welcome! Introduce him to a cotillion of soignée young ladies, yet dutiful to the Muses. And please keep him at a safe distance from Edward Dahlberg, who will berate him for publishing any writers at New Directions other than himself. Kenneth Rexroth always said that 90% of the worst human beings he knew were

*The Steelers won!

poets. "Poets these days are so square they have to walk around the block just to turn over in bed."

*O saeclum insapiens et infacetum!*
What a witless and tasteless age!

*Vale, J!*

*(*Parnassus: Poetry in Review, *Vol. 23, No. 1 & No. 2, 1998)*

# RONALD JOHNSON

# (NOVEMBER 25, 1935-

# MARCH 4, 1998)

In 1973, Guy Davenport wrote in America: "Our greatest living poet is usually a man as unknown to the professariat as to the corps of reviewers and the deaf custodians of the laurels. It was true of Whitman in 1873, and is true of Zukofsky in 1973." Louis Zukofsky (1904–1978) is still not yet canonized and demanded as the Sunday joint at the Muses' dinner table. But those who read beyond the Ivy League Men About Town and the Cornbelt Metaphysicals are aware of his extraordinary skills and his ear for his second language, English. His first was the Yiddish of the slums of the Lower East Side of New York City early in the century.

The poet who replaced LZ in Professor Davenport's pantheon in America was Ronald Johnson, who has just died at the age of 62 in Topeka, Kansas, his native state. The professariat will, again, be absolutely in the dark. And few in Britain will know him either, though he spent years in England in the 1960s and wrote one of the best "English" poems of the time, *The Book of the Green Man*, published by Longmans in 1967.

Ronald Johnson was born November 25th, 1935, in the small, ordinary, artless town of Ashland, in southwestern Kansas. Some of the names of places in that part of the prairie make them more exotic than is the truth: Buttermilk, Bloom, Protection, Acres, Moscow, Ulysses, Liberal, Kismet.

Kismet, Kansas—it's hard to beat. His father managed a lumber yard, as his father had before him. The family moved to Topeka, the state capital. He spent a couple of years at the University of Kansas in nearby Lawrence and concentrated on English courses. He did two years of national service in the Army, in Georgia, Arizona, and California.

I met Ronald Johnson in Washington, DC, at the beginning of 1958. I was using the proceeds of a Guggenheim Foundation grant to read in the Library of Congress for six months, and to publish two early Jargon Society books: *Letters,* by Robert Duncan, and *Overland to the Islands,* by Denise Levertov. One evening I went with the literary critic Marius Bewley to visit a pianist friend who lived on R Street, Northwest, in the house of Mrs. King-Smith, a notable hostess of the time, when the young of the well-to-do were taught dancing and deportment. Another roomer in the house was RJ. He was handsome, red-haired, feisty, ebullient, and clearly very bright. The friendship was immediate, though he was not at all sure that the new book of Denise Levertov I was clutching and showing off contained "real poems."

We joined forces. And I became a mentor, just enough older for that relationship to work. We moved to New York and I worked at the famous 8th Street Bookshop in Greenwich Village, while RJ completed a B.A. degree at Columbia College. We spent a lot of time at the Cedar Bar on University Place with friends like Joel Oppenheimer, Franz Kline, Dan Rice, Fielding Dawson, Gilbert Sorrentino, Esteban Vicente, many of whom I'd known from my earlier days at Black Mountain College. And we visited non-bar-type writers like William Carlos Williams, Louis Zukofsky, and Edward Dahlberg.

I've always liked to play cicerone and to plan itineraries and rambles. In the summer of 1961, RJ and I hiked the Appalachian Trail from Springer Mountain, Georgia, to the Hudson River in New York, some 1447 miles. Perfect training for poets: learning to attend the names of birds and plants and stars and trees and stones. The summer of 1962 I was a writer-in-residence at the Aspen Institute for Humanistic Studies in Colorado; and RJ had his first culinary job, at the *Copper Kettle Restaurant*. In the autumn of 1962 we headed for England and walked five weeks in the Lake District. On the Sunday of the weekend of the Cuban Missile Crisis the poets spent the day trying to locate the graves of Beatrix Potter in Near Sawrey and Kurt Schwitters in Ambleside—and found neither.

We met the extraordinary writer and illustrator Barbara Jones and rented a four-room flat in her house in Well Walk, Hampstead. It was 12 guineas a week! There were parties with friends of Barbara's like Olivia Manning, Kay Dick, and Stevie Smith. We met other London people through our bookseller-friends, John Sandoe, Arthur Uphill, and Bernard Stone: Adrian Mitchell, Mervyn Peake, Christopher Middleton, John Wain, Michael Hamburger, Paul Potts, Anselm Hollo, Christopher Logue, Tom Raworth, Eric Mottram, Rayner Heppenstall, John Heath-Stubbs, R. B. Kitaj, Tom Phillips, Adrian Berg, Andrew Young, Jocelyn Brooke. Barbara's pioneering book, *Follies & Grottoes,* led us all over England and beyond. We went up to Ardgay in Easter Ross in the north of Scotland to meet Ian Hamilton Finlay. We saw Hugh MacDiarmid in both Langholm and Biggar. We saw Basil Bunting up the Tyne above Newcastle at Wylam. And Herbert Read at Stonegrave House in the hills north of York. We went to Broad Town under the Wiltshire Downs to see Geoffrey and Jane Grigson. Geoffrey took us to Faringdon for Lord Berners's folly tower, to Buscot Park for Burne-Jones's *Briar-Rose* paintings, and to Lydiard Tregoze for the splendid interior of the Church of St. Mary. Jane fixed Welsh girdle cakes for breakfast, the first we had ever tasted. We visited the graves of Blake and Palmer, Stanley Spencer and Walter Sickert, Delius and William Morris. In the spring of 1963 we walked from the mouth of the River Wye at Chepstow, up its long, winding valley, to its source high on the flanks of Great Plynlimmon. We hitched a few rides to allow us to add Kilpeck Church to Francis Kilvert's at Bredwardine along the route. And Strata Florida and the site of Hafod House further into Wales. And more pilgrimages that summer. To Nottinghamshire to Southwell Minster and the amazing foliate heads and plant carvings in the Chapter House. To Gilbert White's Selborne in Hampshire. To Samuel Palmer's Shoreham in Kent. To the Cerne Abbas Giant in Dorset. To Compton in Surrey for the Watts Mortuary Chapel. To Brighton for John Nash's Royal Pavilion. We were looking for all things, as RJ said, "most rich, most glittering, most strange."

And we kept on looking. In the autumn of 1965 we were back in England. One hike took us from Land's End along the north coast of Cornwall, Devon, and Somerset. We ended it in the Cheddar Gorge, where we discovered the Rev. Toplady had once composed "Rock of Ages." Someone told us about The Miner's Arms, a pub at Priddy, where an ex-academic (Paul Leyton) was serving very good food. We walked on to Priddy and found this to be true. There were snails from the Mendip Hills on the menu. And Priddy Oggy. What that was I have forgotten. The name is unforgettable . . . Another six months in London. This time only a two-room flat chez Barbara Jones at 7 guineas a week. One night we invited William Burroughs and R. Buckminster Fuller to dinner and neither knew who the other was—just a couple of old Harvard men. RJ produced a Shaker lemon pie for afters and Burroughs muttered: "Hey, man, that is the craziest lemon pie. I mean groovy!" Since two pies had been baked, RJ wrapped the second one up and El Hombre Invisible took it home with him.

In the spring of 1966 the U.S. Information Agency set up a tour for me to read my *Mahler* poems in six Austrian cities and that allowed us to go also to Bruckner and Webern sites and many rococo churches and palaces. We drove down through the Dolomites to Milan Airport and picked up two friends from Georgia who had hired us to transport them around Italy and France. With three months in hand we saw much on the tourist routes, but we added a few delicacies: the Villa Lante, the Garden of the Monsters at Bomarzo, the cemeteries in Milan and Genoa. And in France, the Parisian cemeteries, the Pique-Assiette House in Chartres, the Ideal Dream Palace of the Postman Cheval in Hauterives. The latter we saw after lunching at Fernand Point's *Restaurant de la Pyramide* in Vienne, the best food any of us had ever tasted.

In 1967 I was back at the Aspen Institute as a scholar-in-residence. RJ worked again at the *Copper Kettle*. Things were about to change. Our companionship of nearly a decade was always much more peripatetic than restricted and passionate. Roving legs meant roving eyes. When RJ realized I was tired of living in cities, he packed his bags one day and got a ride to San Francisco with some mysterious amoroso. He was 32 years old and wanted more space between himself and the perils of rustic living and Kansas, the Sunflower State.

He led a hand-to-mouth existence in San Francisco for about 25 years and we saw each other very rarely. He would report that he was bartending in a club for bikers and leather boys; or, that he had established a little catering business. He published a few poetry books and four excellent cookbooks: *The American Table, Simple Fare, Company Fare,* and *New & Old Southwestern Cooking. The American Table* is a classic work, right up there with M. F. K. Fisher at her best. Occasionally he would get a semester's teaching job: at the University of Kentucky in 1971; at the University of Washington in 1973; at Stanford University in 1991; and at the University of California, Berkeley, in 1994. Now and then he would be helped financially by stalwart friends like Donald B. Anderson, Dorothy Neal, James Laughlin, Gus Blaisdell, and Guy Davenport.

For over twenty years Ronald Johnson composed and fitted together an architectonic poem in 99 sections called *Ark*. It is in the traditions of Ezra Pound, Charles Olson, Louis Zukofsky, and Robert Duncan. It is a formidable achievement and it will require readers not easily daunted, who have untrammeled imaginations. Thom Gunn and Robert Creeley are two of *Ark*'s champions. They both point out that this is an aesthetic work, not a didactic one, and there is much pleasure to be gained. William Blake is there; the Land of Oz is there; the Bible is there; Simon Rodia's Watts Towers are there. An edition of *Ark* was published in 1996 by the Living Batch Press of Albuquerque, New Mexico. It is distributed through the University of New Mexico Press, 1720 Lomas Boulevard NE, Albuquerque, NM 87131-1591, USA.

Here, at the end, I want to bring your attention back to Ronald Johnson's *The Book of the Green Man*. Christopher Middleton instigated the book's publication and on the front flap said: "This is the work of a young poet from Kansas who spent a year in England during 1962–63. It is a remarkable piece of work. The surprise is this: he presents an image of England, or, to be precise, of sundry English scenes, with a vividness and strangeness beyond the reach of any English poet, and unknown, I venture to say, since the days of Blake, Calvert and Palmer. Ronald Johnson has unearthed an England which most people have forgotten." At the end of the Autumn section, the four seasons are over. The poet is at Samuel Palmer's Shoreham in Kent. The composer Wilfrid Mellers wrote a beautiful multi-voiced canticle based on the ecstatic reverie with which *The Book of the Green Man* concludes:

> *I walked up to the CLOUD,*
>
> *'a country*
> *where there is no*
> *night'*
>
> *but of moons*
> *& with heads of fish*
>
> *in the furrow*
>
> *& on each*
> *ear, beneath a husk*
> *of twilight*
>
> *were as many suns as*
> *kernels,*
>
> *& fields were far*

as the eye
could reach.

Then dipping their silver oars,

the eyes
shed characters of fire
in the grain,

its sheaves as if mackerel
shone on the waves

of air.


I walked up to the CLOUD

& the white light
opened
like flowers—


dog violets,
& asphodel, celandine,

red clover.


I walked up to the CLOUD

& peal after peal
rang out of earth.

First, stones
underfoot
in a sound like muffled

sheep-bells.
Then the roots of the trees

*clanged:*
*rooks, rooks, blackbirds. Cuckoos awoke*
*in the tubers*

*—earth-worm & mole & turtle—*

*all danced to the thunder,*
*the peal & thunder.*

*A bellow & clamor*
*came out*
*of the hills:*

*in diapason—a dissonance*
*& musical order.*


ROOKS, ROOKS, BLACK-
BIRDS, CUCKOOS.

EARTH-WORM & MOLE
& TURTLE.


A YELLOW MOON, A YELLOW MOON, A YELLOW MOON.
Scents of newly-cut wheat
billow on the night air. An owl
calls—echoes & reverberates around us.
Dimness & brilliance meet.
Large stars.

*(* The Independent, *London, March 18, 1998)*

# JAMES HAROLD JENNINGS
## (APRIL 20, 1931–APRIL 20, 1999)

I was at a garage in Pinnacle, North Carolina, getting the mechanics to look after some ghastly rattle under the VW Rabbit. So I asked: "Do you fellers know a local man named James Harold Jennings?" "Red Jennings, why sure! Listen, Red's a sight-and-a-half. Lived here all his life. His mother left him a right nice farm out there on Purch Road. How come you know him?" "Well, he's a very good artist. I like those things he makes." "Oh yeah, well, I wouldn't know about that art stuff. Used to see him a lot, he'd come by on his bicycle, pickin' up bottles and cans along the road." "Well, now, he makes art out of scrap wood and stuff. You ought to go have a look. Many thanks for your help, boys."

It's such a common story. The boys down at the garage, they haven't paid attention to James Harold—or anybody else "strange"—for a month of Sundays. If a person's strange-harmless, there's still just about enough room in rural America for him to be left alone. Scare the neighbors, and it's off to the funny farm or the pokey. It's two protective miles from the garage southwest to the "Art World of James Harold Jennings."

By now, there are four orange and yellow decrepit school and bible-church buses clustered by the road, intermixed with jerrybuilt structures like miniature tobacco barns. Every day, including Sunday, you will find the Artist of the Sun, the Moon, and the Stars, always at home and hard at work, cutting up plywood and painting, making his unique pieces. James Harold's constant companions are ten or so cats. He used to live across the road in the old family house. Now he chooses to live in one of the buses, that way the cats don't have to cross the road and risk getting killed by the car jockeys who speed by.

James Harold tells his visitors that he enjoys living "kind of low," like the Amish people, in the old style. He has no running water, or electricity, or car, or telephone, or tv. He sleeps on a pallet in the yellow bus, upon which he unrolls an old sleeping bag. He goes to bed when it gets dark and gets up when it's light. He has a kerosene stove on which to prepare his simple meals. He likes country ham, pinto beans, vienna sausages, saltine crackers, canned chicken and dumplings, and coffee. I imagine he must make a little corn pone now and then in the skillet. While he works outside on his art, he listens to country music on his portable radio, smokes Hav-a-Tampa cigars, and enjoys Miller Sandwiches. "Miller Sandwiches—what are those, James Harold?" "Boys, that's when you take two Miller beers and put a third in between 'em."

What to say about James Harold? I would venture to say that he is one of the most charming and delightful artists in the world. An equal, say, to Joan Miro. He's endlessly inventive and the pieces have a rare lilt and twang about them. And here he is, working away almost unknown in Stokes County, about 25 minutes north of Winston-Salem. Luckily he lives at the "country end" of his road. Around Mr. Jennings a few people still live in log cabins and keep tobacco barns. The closer you get to the city the more gentrified the houses are becoming. They have decorated mail boxes, some of them, but the usual flying geese and ploughs and minstrel show jockeys—nothing quite so wild as J. H. "Red" Jennings, the "crazy" man down the road.

James Harold votes Republican but doesn't like George Bush or that ornery sumbitch, Jesse Helms, he's just afraid the Democrats will ban all tobacco products—and what else can a poor man find for enjoyment but a smoke and a beer or three?

What does he make? Brightly colored scrap-wood constructions painted with enamel and day-glo latex. Some are ferris wheels, some are whirligigs, some are like shooting gallery constructions, or like billboards, or Burma Shave signs along the old highways (HARDLY A MAN IS NOW ALIVE/WHO CROSSED A HILL AT 75), or tableaux, featuring processions of pussy cats and dinosaurs; rough, tough women beating on little male bullies and devils. "Ah-MAY-zahn women," James Harold calls them.

> tufgh women are the thing now
>
> people want
> judy tames a bully
> carla tames a bully
> charlotte tames a bully
> bessie tames a bully
>
> some want 'em side-saddle
> some want 'em on top
> little bottom men
>
> top people
> even lawyers
> doctors professors dentists want
> great big old mean
> tufgh women

Though he only went through five years of grade school, James Harold is a prodigious reader. He has stacks of *Popular Mechanics* and *National Geographic* magazines, plus books on astral projection, electroencephalography, and metempsychosis—"them's dictionary words, boys." Back in 1986, James Harold told Steve Litt, reporter for *The Raleigh News & Observer*, about some of his sources:

What truth there is in the Bible is astrology. You can get down on your knees and pray for what you want to, and, if it comes, it comes, but it won't come from God.

James Harold Jennings says his work is often inspired by religion—but not the mainstream kind. He believes in The Goddess. Which one, he's not sure. It might be Diana, the Roman moon goddess; or, Lillith, the mythical creature who preceded Eve in the Garden of Eden.

He began after the death of his mother, who'd taught him, as he says, all he needed to know about the outside world. His father, a veterinarian, died when he was three. I was visiting with James Harold the other day when two collectors from Michigan drove in. There were dazzled and delighted by what they saw. One of them, Richard Ginger, a blueberry grower from Bangor, Michigan, asked James Harold: "How long have you been at it; and, how come you started to paint and make things?" The answer was very simple and very moving. He said it was about eight years ago, and: "Well, boys, you know there's a whole lot of company in what I do. I never ever get lonely . . . That's because my art is somethin' they call visionary art."

To this point you have been reading excerpts of a portrait of James Harold Jennings in an unpublished book of mine called *Walks to the Paradise Garden*, with photographs by Roger Manley and Guy Mendes. And now we come to 1999 and lapse into the past tense. Early on the morning of April 20th, his 68th birthday, James Harold put a pistol to his head and shot himself. This was the same April 20th when the Trenchcoat Mafia were celebrating the 110th birthday of Adoph Hitler in Littleton, Colorado, by killing 14 high school students and a teacher. Though James Harold had said "I never get lonely," his sister-in-law, Normie Jennings, tells me that recently he was being treated for depression and was taking medicine. He seemed very nervous and agitated by the coming of the Millennium, and afraid that vandals and lawless mobs would come and wreck his Art World. Y2K has claimed an early victim, a sadly vulnerable one, celebrated as yet only by the world of Outsider Art.

Hoist a "Miller Sandwich" and toast James Harold with a fond farewell. It was William Carlos Williams who said that "the pure products of America go crazy." No longer true. Half the people you see today look scary, on tv, at the mall, or driving around like bats out of hell. And there are 250,000,000 handguns in the USA, at least one for every citizen.

(The Independent, London, May 5, 1999)

# HARRY CALLAHAN

## ON HAGURO-SAN

A letter from Russell Edson, the fabulist, invariably contains some sombre reminder: "There's always next year, until there's not. I don't think we would need to take our shoes off to count them."

So, now the obituary pages of *The New York Times* give us Harry Morey Callahan (1912–1999), photographer, born in Detroit. Gone. Damnation! "Gone into what/ like all them kings/ you read about," to quote a fragment of e.e. cummings' beautiful elegy for Sam Ward, the handyman at Silver Lake. Gone. And, Harry, me boyo, I wanted to tell you at least one more vintage Irish joke: "Why did the Irishman keep an empty bottle of milk in the fridge? In case anybody asked for black coffee." C'est sublime...

I was blessed with an extraordinary collection of mentors: Harry Callahan, Aaron Siskind, Frederick Sommer, Henry Holmes Smith, Clarence John Laughlin, Raymond Moore; Stefan Wolpe, Harry Partch, Lou Harrison; Kenneth Rexroth, Kenneth Patchen, Edward Dahlberg, Charles Olson, Paul Goodman, Robert Duncan, Geoffrey Grigson, Basil Bunting, and James Laughlin. Lou Harrison is the only one remaining among us—active and vital at 82 in Aptos, California. You think about these things when you hit the Big-Seven-O. Just two weeks ago I scaled the stupendous heights of Gehenna or Tophet, whichever it was, and

240

walking over the bonehills, I entered the portals of Genuine Geezerhood. Basil Bunting asserted very firmly that poets over 70 should be summarily ground into cat's meat. So, I have less than 350 days to dance and sing, friends and neighbors.

I've pulled 12 Callahan books off the shelves and I've spent some two hours ruminating, looking at the images and reading some of the texts. I had never noticed before this perceptive writing by Keith Davis in *Harry Callahan: New Color (Photographs 1978–1987)*, published by Hallmark Cards, Inc. "Proficiency in both golf and photography depends on sensitivity, balance, timing, and precision . . . Both require an inward focussing of attention, and the ability to simultaneously think and feel one's way through the process . . . In both disciplines successful "shots" are, to some degree, mysterious and unpredictable . . . And both activities are deceptively complex; they are easy to do, but exceedingly difficult to do well." Harry used to shoot in the 70's. Good for him! As for photography, he said he'd maybe shot 40,000 images and liked 800.

Gertrude Stein said that when a Jew dies, he's dead. With Catholics, it's something else. *Laudamus te, benedicimus te!* Early on, Harry Callahan said: "A picture is like a prayer; you're offering a prayer to get something, and in a sense it's like a gift of God because you have practically no control—at least I don't." In a photograph by Todd Webb (1945) Harry looks very monkish. His reticence all his life aims toward the Cistercians, and maybe even the Trappists. Who knows? How eloquent he was when he said things like: "I love art because it doesn't have rules like baseball. The only rule is to be good. That's the toughest thing to do." Do the job, keep quiet. It was Jean de LaFontaine who noted: "By the work one knows the workman."

Harry also said that after he'd encountered Ansel Adams at a workshop in Detroit in 1941 he realized there were no mountains in Michigan, so he would have to look very hard at the ground under his feet. He loved walking. So, imagination makes me want to put him into a distant landscape with Matsuo Basho.

It's 1689 and Basho, the greatest of Japanese haiku poets, is about to set forth from Edo (old Tokyo) on an 800 mile walk to the Sacred Mountains with Sora, his friend and disciple. Time for Harry Callahan to change his garments, stick a 35mm camera and a 4 x 5 view camera into his knapsack, master Japanese on the jet from Atlanta, bow to the Master, and call himself Sora. Let's listen to a few things they will say along *The Narrow Road to the Deep North.* I am using Cid Corman's translation of the text for the Basho. He comments: "We too move out with him to and through the backwater regions of Honshu. His words are our provision, breath, rhythm. And they can never be not of our time. The end of his journey is the end of ours. Everywhere he goes one feels a sounding made, the ground hallowed, hardwon, endeared to him, and so to us, through what others had made of it, had reached, discovered." The information about Haguro-san I glean from the sagacious Jonathan Greene.

Basho: "O glorious / green leaves young leaves' / sun light"

Harry: "Michigan, 1912 / my parents were farmers / no art, but / father liked music: / Caruso records"

Basho: "fleas lice / horse pishing / by the pillow"

Harry: "I was going to be like Van Gogh / never be recognized / and do this great stuff"

Basho: "quiet / into rock absorbing / cicada sounds"

Harry: "I never knew what I was doing, / so how come you think you know?"

Basho: "cruel! / under the helmet / cricket"

Harry: "some talk about / Far-Eastern thought; / I guess mine's / Mid-Western"

Basho: "cool ah / faint crescent's / Haguro-san"

Harry: "when I went there, it was with my heart, / and I felt that they came with their hearts"

**242**

We leave our poet and photographer on Haguro-san (along with Gassan and Yuduro-san), one of the "Three Mountains of Dewa," sacred to mountain ascetics known as Yamabushi. Past a famous five-story pagoda there are 2,446 stone steps up the mountain through very old straight & tall cedar trees. I hope to see you both there one day.

(Aperture 156, New York, 1999)